The Peach Pit Mask

A Poetry Collection

SAMMI YAMASHIRO

This is a work of creative nonfiction. Some parts have been fictionalized in varying degrees, for various purposes.

First paperback edition 2021

Front cover art by Sammi Yamashiro

ISBN 978-1-7368502-0-6 (paperback)

For my two best friends.
You two have believed in me for years and have urged me to write what I could never carry vocally. For the next Einstein and Tesla: I love you, I love you.

For my high school English teachers.
All of you begged me to publish at least one book in my life. So, here it is.

For the online poetry community.
I would not be alive today if it weren't for you.
Now, I return the favor.

For those who need the peach pits,
carry this mask with you.

CONTENTS

"The question, O me! So sad, recurring—
What good amid these, O me, O life?

Answer.
That you are here— that life exists and identity;
That the powerful play goes on,
And you will contribute a verse."

Walt Whitman

SEARCHING FOR AND RECLAIMING MY VOICE | 2017

AGES 15 & 16

MY FATHER AND THIS DREADFUL WORLD TRIED THEIR BEST TO MUTE ME AND BELITTLE MY EFFORTS.
I AM NO WEAKLING.
THE REST OF YOU WERE HANDED RESPECT WITH NO ATTEMPT ON YOUR PART. I EARNED IT.
LET ME INDULGE ON MY RESULTS.

Impermanence

May 7, 2017

I awoke one Saturday
To the loudest of pours.
I swung my heavy arms to bend the blinds
And with laden eyes, I saw war:
The concrete floor turned to river,
The sky, a shade of platinum.
I could not see for miles, not even a sliver,
I was amidst a pure tantrum.

I, then, returned to sleep,
As I was still weary.
When I cracked my eyes, again, to greet,
I thought my eyes could not see clearly:
Gentle sunshine filled my room
And I looked to the window to see
Thinning cotton clouds sucked of gloom,
And the lack of puddles caused by heat.
Most importantly, there was a stillness in the air,
As if the sky felt numb from the tears it had fared.

All of this made me realize
that moments and feelings are temporary.
Like how a storm can swing by,
It can also disappear and bury.
Afterwards, happiness says hello,
But it can take a while to reply at last:
The scars the storm left on you are not mellow,
And they do not heal quite fast.
Yet once you begin to embrace happiness,
You shall give the universe a brave kiss.
And yes, the rain will surely come again,
And it could fester to a storm, too,
But once you remember that the downpour will drain,
You will know that temporariness is true.

Humanity's Sonnet

May 12, 2017

When we escape our mother's womb,
We are born to spread hate;
We are destined to doom.
Why is this our fate?

We think greed is just,
Like the six other sins.
We all have it in us,
You can't deny it.

I'm mad to assume
That we are only that.
Within us we store cures,
And the harmonies of laugh!

Flawed but beautiful us.
This is life, before we are dust.

The Scab and Its Sonnet

May 13, 2017

When have you shown me love?
You are enraged when I am distant,
But you act like you are not the same.

Do you not understand?
You left me permanent scars;
I shudder at the sound of your voice
From all the times you made me feel worthless.
The hours upon hours of hollers you shoved at me
Left me these scabs which read:

I am mentally weak
And constantly on guard.
I am a child at heart, permanently.
You have strangled me hard.
All those nights I wanted to dream,
You would keep me up
So you could torture me
And suffocate the 'young'.
All I wanted was your satisfaction,
A reason for me to live;
Maybe I was your distraction
From looking into the crib.
    To this day, you're still the same;
    How delusional, how deranged.

The Realization

MAY 16, 2017

On this accidental weekend,
It all hit me in one pounding blow:

It isn't just him who does not love me—
No one does.
I'm shunned for being silent,
But it's just that they don't see
That in my own life, it's so violent.
My thoughts are never wiped clean.
I thought I had my allies.
I thought they loved me, too.
Yet, it seems I am forgotten.

They have said goodbye oh so soon.

The Trees Sprout with No Care in The World

MAY 19, 2017

My limbs are a forest
Stretching from head to toe.
From a mile away and even the closest,
The trees sprout with no care in the world.

Some days, I like to free my skin
And stray from skin-tight jeans.
Those days I show what I feel within
With the risk of glaring fiends.

I spy judgement from the corner of your eye,
And in return, I pay with a grin,
Because why must I let your ignorant cry
Be the wall to stifle my hymn?

These trees, we say, should never be grown,
So I should be an alien for letting them show.
But why should my beauty be diminished,
When I am only being natural, a hushed sin?

Obligations

MAY 20, 2017

The love you hand me is material
And material, I feel.
At the end of every day,
I can't feel a love unreal.

Indeed, you pay me gold and chains,
And at first, I was fulfilled;
But my heart knows more than my own brain
And it knows that paper bills can't fill
This desolate, barren,
And incredibly vast
Crate,
Which nestles deep into my gentle heart.

Am I obligated to love you,
When I know you'll never fill my void?

He Cries Because He Has To

MAY 21, 2017

Our masculinity dies when we cry.
At least that's what we're told
By our peers, by mom and dad,
By the rule book signed with our names.
But the truth and the fact is—
It takes the strongest person to finally crack,
And the weakest to mock him.

To My Future Lovers

MAY 21, 2017

My first love, my second, and the ones after them;
My soulmate, my meant-to-be's, and the ones
who will leave,
I want more than infatuation; I want to comprehend
your being.
I want to dissect your soul and analyze its energy.
I want to surround your winters with a shelter warmed
by fire.
I want to see the reality of the hope that is higher.

Most importantly, I hope you want the same, future lover.

The City of Hope

JUNE 4, 2017

On the day before my sixteenth birthday, several people died in the 2017 London Bridge terrorist attack. I wrote this wondering why I still got to live and celebrate another year in my life when all I wanted was to die.

In the city where hopes are met,
Where the busy live to thrive,
Where kings and queens once sat,
Where children, and their children, will rise—
The children, with dreams in their eyes,
Walk with purpose to make dreams reality.
They hustle to subways to seize the day
And skip across the platforms, waiting for their trains...

White light.
A sharp pain on the side.
Bombs, bullets, and fragments of metal
Slice deep into the skin of the innocent,
But before they realize it,
All they can do is lay dazed and
Smell, with heightened senses, a wave of iron.
They taste the putrid smoke, swallow it whole,
And exhale their life and some gunpowder.
Their ears detect the next round of shells.
One... Four? Six? Seven...
Lost count.
One inch too close steals another beating heart;
One inch too far steals the pair of dreaming eyes.
One less human, one less joy;
A city once hopeful, now destroyed.

Cycle

JUNE 22, 2017

Point me to a path;
guide me to a sign;
attach some training wheels to my bike.
Let me know that I can smoothly ride!
Any time there's a road heading straight
I always seem to steer a little late.
There's a forest up ahead that I'd like to see
but it turns out it's not what it appears to be.
Why must uncertainty cloud my mind
when I should aim for what I strive?
I have only one chance to experience me,
so why can't I erase the doubt and let the wheels free?

Sea Similarities

JUNE 25, 2017

Some of us are like the sea:
from a distance, we reflect the sun.
We feed on the energy and bounce it off.
A closer look and we find
a glittering exterior, so divine.
The sun rays make us shimmer.
If we dare touch, we will quiver.

Yet, if we dive in the vast sea
we will notice it is hard to open our eyes.
Once we do, the salt stings our might.
Through blurry vision we will see
some plastic litter beneath seaweed.
Forgotten trash makes home here,
but the inhabitants make it queer.
The ocean isn't so beautiful now,
but the ocean isn't to blame:

Fishers abuse us, use us,
forcing us to eat these plastic lies.
It will take many light years
for the landfill to die.
If others attempt to clean it,
then maybe the sea will shine from within.

The Every Knight

ORIGINALLY WRITTEN JUNE 25, 2017

The original version was two lines long and quite lifeless. The version presented here is a rework from 2019.

Always I fear you will walk through the front again:
I hear the clatter of keys twist the lock,
and with it, your damned footsteps...
Something swills my conscious, and I cease;
I hyperventilate, slipping a reverb.
My glycerin torso crumples under my bed sheets,
and I melt.

I am my breath; you touch it plainly.
(I was never great at hide-and-seek.)
"Common sense!" For once you already knew.
You expel my blood, not a bond.
The sabotage executes itself like the night acting as the day.
I beg, all I ask is to sleep!

The Sun Has Almost Left

JULY 6, 2017

My first published poem.

In this block of cement
where impermanence lives,
there are brief little visits
of the light's sun kiss.

It happens 'round mid noon:
The blinds create their stripes,
the sun rays sting the dirty windows
and unveil some floating life.
With it, silence brews.
Ah...
Silence...

In a home where chaos is constant,
the quiet is the blanket that lulls me to sleep.
It's the calm before the inevitable storm.
I shut my eyes to shield the nightmare dream,
but this barrier, so paper thin, can only do so much for me.

Behind Curtains of Laughter

JULY 11, 2017

I am slowly fading.
My insides are brittle; my heart, a glass
draining all the joy out of me, drop by plop.
My brain is exhausted from battle.
It's been drafted into this war, fighting for a
moment of delight.
I disguise all of this behind curtains of laughter.
I make light of my agony, and so do you.
Feel no guilt, my friend.
This is how I've grown to deal with hardship:
Suppress all emotion,
or wear a painful grin.

Your Change

JULY 18, 2017

I watch from afar of the changes friends make:
they sing different songs, and they chase the wrong bait.
Yesterday, in a past life, we would kiss, laugh, and balter.
Today, another phase, we lie in facades and falter.

I swear only hours ago
we were carving oaths in our skin,
promising to never give in.
Viridity clouded our minds,
thinking we'd never see demise.

Seeing my loved ones conform
makes me question why some things are the norm.
Growth is needed, I know,
but why must it be this path?

Where is the innocence that once was them?
Who injected this hurt of venom?

*viridity – innocence, youth, naivety

It's All Up to You

August 7, 2017

A pro, a con;
Every decision, twist in a maze,
Comes with these two, hand in hand.
You must weigh them out;
decide which path is worth the scrapes
and worth the night and worth the day.
Roll towards that kind of will.

Outdo that howl.
Then pursue, pursue it.

Slave

SEPTEMBER 9, 2017

I'm his slave.
Every sunrise is a new day,
a new pain to fight away.
I try to claim victor with my own battles,
but he takes a swing while my guard is down.

My heart beats down my rib cage
when I sense his presence a thousand miles away.
"Did I do something wrong again?"
I say as I stir the bloody meat. Its iron stings my nostrils.
He takes a deep breath...
then...
he begins to roar like a demon possessed him.
I feel all of yesterday's, today's, and tomorrow's anxieties
travel to the bottom of my eyes,
filling a bath.
My mind stops functioning, my breathing quickens.
"Stop crying over the food! I don't want to get sick!"
Is the tagline he screeches.

But a waterfall doesn't halt to convenience a captain.
Certainly not for a captain.

It's the same dilemma every day.

And I swear, I swear I try to make his day!
Satisfy his every need and numb his heartache!
But it's no use; the cause of *this* explosion is me, me.
He'll pass so young because of myself, myself.
"You are... You can't... You stop..." You. Me.
I am just a slave who will never please.

I Want... But I Chase After...

SEPTEMBER 9, 2017

Sometimes I wonder: do I really know what I want?
I say I long for a friend, a partner-in-crime,
who isn't only there for giggles and small talk
but chats with me for hours
about the fate of our future,
the artificial ideals of our society,
and what we look for in true love;
what *is* true love and how do we deal with heartbreak?

Even so,
I still blindly pick and choose
the people who should care the most.
A lot of them throw me out to a landfill when they've had enough.
With each visit, I grow smaller,
rottener.
There's always that starving pigeon
who lands next to me, nibbling my veins and arteries,

interrupting my pulse.

Twelve

SEPTEMBER 11, 2017

She was so pure and simple; she was blinded by the fog;
the child who believed that all marriages are love.
Her mother had a box of fragrant white carnations,
which she gifted to her lover in a moonlit view location.

Her mom and dad, inseparable, sealed their promise
with a kiss.
The child thought that she, herself, was evidence of this.
When the child soon turned twelve, she finally took notice
that her mother's eyes were a spilling glass when she
locked eyes with him.

Then one fateful night,
a full moon hid behind swift clouds.
The girl trembled,
inhaled violent breaths,
and crushed her ears with her nimble palms.
Her father, right next door,
had her mother's neck tangled in his hands.
All the girl could hear was:
"Where are they? Where are they? I won't let go till you
tell me!"

It felt like decades flew by when her father stormed out
the house.
The girl came to her mommy's aid and sobbed in
mother's arms.
How could he be so cruel? How could he bruise your
shoulders?
How could he pull you close to death? He sees your
gemmed ring finger!

"No, I was the one who hurt him."
There stood a perennial frost between her and her mother.
"I gave the box of carnations to somebody else," her
mother finally whispered.
"But... those flowers... are made of plastic...
They were never real..."

When the sun peeked out again,
the girl stood in front of her mirror.
She suddenly appeared quite different
from the person that she thought she knew.
The gold shined on her dulling skin,
her under eyes painted jet black.
Breakfast had tasted so bland and bitter,
and her teeth were fragile; they could crack.
Most of all, her mind was vacant,
and it probably weighed an ounce.

The woman plodded to her muddy window,
and saw not blue skies, but clouds.

The Land of the Rising Sun

SEPTEMBER 11, 2017

My first tanka which, for me, captures the bliss of waking up during a Japanese summer morning. I was terribly homesick, which may have prompted me to write this.

A summer morning,
it begins like no other:
The red sun rises,
and spells another heatwave.
We cicadas thrive in it.

Last Priority

SEPTEMBER 11, 2017

An adaptation of a song I had written two years prior.

So, this is 'lonely'.
Who could have known how much it stings
to have your trusted companions dismiss you so easily?
Even the most casual hello turns into a heated debate.

I don't know what I do wrong!
I'm quite genuinely confused.
Maybe my choice of conversation
causes the world to go aloof?

(It's mind boggling still: I talk about my craving for plums and I spot her hissing in disgust. Does she hate plums?)

The ones that I thought loved me,
I'm now their last priority.
Even if I act hysterical
(They must want me to:
I act as interesting as a blank paper),
All I am is last place, a forgettable name.

Why do I even bother anymore?
Why should I even try?
All that's left is to talk to the wind because at least the wind replies!

I lie in my bed with my eyes peeling,
wondering if I'll live to see another sunset,
because really, and I mean really,
why?
Why should I?

Never Was Yours

SEPTEMBER 22, 2017

I've been yanked by my hair,
which fell off my head.
I've been burned at the stake:
blue flames licking my skin.
I've been skinned raw:
food for fruit flies who feast.

I've drunken out of wine glasses
poured in with brown blood.
I've been dared to drink the ocean,
then covered in mud.

I've seen it all.
I've died, been buried alive,
been a body of seventy percent dirt, not water.

I'm sick
of being controlled
by mere threads,
by puppeteers
who will never let go.

I.
Am.
Done.

I will take your beloved scissors
and slice those strings right off.
I am not a doll with no soul.
I am not an abstract form whose fate you control.
The rules of the game you make me play
are now just flames boiling in my veins.

I am sick of your 'pity'.
Your silicone tears can rot in Hell.
Those lies you spoon-fed me,
I'll regurgitate back at you when you tell...

No,
don't tell.
I won't hear you say another word.
I'll venture on my own,
without your white noise.
Don't go down on your knees,
begging.
You'll just kill energy.

I don't need you,
and I never did.

To be Afraid to Glance

September 25, 2017

My vision whitens;
my retinas sizzle;
I can feel the cataracts developing in my naked eyes.

Hottest of the hottest
summer day,
will the heavens bequeath me
a guarded gate?

Fire bubbles in my eyes.
I divert to the shade
of the lonely palm tree.

My skin should feel like snow,
because snow means pure and normal.
But my fingers graze the surface of my skin
and they pop and crackle and drip.

I'm burning alive!
My hand! My fingers!

I'm too afraid to look at the damage,
the damage of the sun.
But how could I avoid this agony in my body!

So, I peeked:
My fingers are melting gold,
trickling down my hands,
which are colored with cocoa.

To my complete and utter surprise,
it doesn't smell like a burning house.
It's more of a homesickness, a nostalgia.
The liquid rolls to the soil,
highlighting the entire tree.
I retreat under it and run my hands through the roots
as we watch the sun collapse to sleep.

No Gray

SEPTEMBER 29, 2017

You see in contrasting black and white.
No inkling of a color gray.
You are even worse than Hollywood.

You are nothing more than machinery.
Consume what they have told and nothing more.
Spit out the feed! Wasting our energy.
Box lights are fevered, the cameras on you.
But no action, no action from you.
Everything is melting, but we hand green to TV.

Must I replace your eyes with mine? With hers? With his?
You shoved your empathy down to the heated core of Earth.
But even she won't allow herself to digest your needed nutrients.

Light does not bounce on your eye.
Simplicity sees in black and white.

Does It Feel Good?

OCTOBER 17, 2017

Another burning candle.
You are not here to celebrate.

Again.

"I'm busy paying the bills."
I know that's true.

Yet, when you have time,
you go run with the gangs to new adventures instead.

When you are strapped to a chair,
you are never smiling.
You roll your eyes,
staring at your ticking watch,

waiting till the long hand reaches twelve.

Now, I'm all yours.
You abuse that delicious power.
You prod and manipulate my mushy brain.

Does it feel good?

I Am I

OCTOBER 22?, 2017

I am I.

I do not belong to him.
I am not handcuffed to him.
My destiny is not determined by him.
My heart pumps to keep me going, not him.
My heart springs for him, but not only for him.
If he ever tries to own me, I won't let him.
He must kill his obsession before it turns into possession.

I hold responsibility for my own internal utopia,
And yes, I am very much capable.

For I belong to me,
And you belong to you.
No one belongs to anyone.

We coincide with one another,
But we are separate entities.
For you are you
and I am I.

The Night I Left

NOVEMBER 3, 2017

Written on my last night of living in the Marshall Islands, where I lived for a year. Here I write of the few beauties that existed there, even though much of my time there contained traumatic events.

My eyes shrivel from exhaust;
they're covered in ghostly salt.
I take the time to turn off the lights anyway,
and creak open the window to watch this life fade.
I see past the blank canvas of houses which guard me
and tilt my head high and embody the galaxy far beyond the seas.
The star fire from eight years before enters my iris;
there won't be another star dust mess like this.

I float atop jagged rocks where the ocean slices.
The city of life seems within arm's reach,
but it's too far. If I attempt to reach now, I'll drown.
For now, I'll listen to the ocean's cries
underneath the starlight.
No! Someone took me by the ends of my hair!
I must leave now and wave solemnly to my lair.
Goodbye deathly sea, farewell colorful Hollywood overhead!
I'll miss you most of all, galaxy, for you are unable to come with.

A New Millennium

NOVEMBER 15?, 2017

Our wrists are pinned to webs,
but we have knives for teeth.

Cocoons were born to shed.
We tinker greener said's!

Throw out our redundancy!
Expose it vulnerable, no longer curious nor a gem.

Rid of constancy!
Seek innovation!

As glimmering glass eyes,
urge Earth to feel surprised.

Half-breed

DECEMBER 12?, 2017

This may have been the first piece I wrote when I moved back home to Okinawa and attended my third high school, a private Christian school.
I was an atheist among a group of religious teenagers, and I wasn't very welcomed there; neither did my home life improve very much.

I.

Every child who has ever poured a fountain of oxygen in their heart, veins, and lungs
is born holding an angel in one hand, a phantom: the other.
All of us carry the ability to tickle our faces with sun rays,
or singe and lacerate ourselves raw to boil in bubbles under it.

I wonder if God and Lucifer came together to birth that cryptic child,
me.
Born with a soft angel caressing my fingers.
Born with a phantom possessing me of all sense and decision.

I want to shield everyone from the chainsaw severing our civilization.

I control that same chainsaw.
Not out of angst, but out of my selfish need to see a scarlet portrait on that hoary wall.
I'm desperate to see color, even if iron fumes bloom from the masterpiece.

II.

I could name the most diseased adjectives in every form of communication,
enunciate every
vowel,
consonant,
vowel,
flick them against my grinding teeth,
and still, none of them could capture my essence very well.

*hoary – grayish white

NUMBNESS ALL THROUGHOUT... YET, I HAD FOUND GOD | 2018

AGES 16 & 17

I RETURN TO MY MOTHER, BUT SHE WANTS LITTLE TO DO WITH ME. I AM ROOTLESS. I AM NOT A PORCELAIN CUP; I AM THE VACANCY INSIDE IT, THE SEE-THROUGH AIR. WHO COULD EVER LOVE A USELESSNESS SUCH AS THAT?
GOD. HE HELD ME IN HIS PALMS ALL ALONG.

Lost at Sea Without A Reason to Breathe

January 1, 2018

Lost at sea without a reason to breathe,
I am stolen by currents headed nowhere.
Grabbed by a hurricane during defeat,
Hauled through sea salt, gasping for air, I
Taste the madness the ocean bears.

I must be going insane as well... but that does
Not have to be bad news. A

Dozen centuries later, I
Am a mermaid. I have learned to navigate Earth's
Rivers and her seven oceans, but I still ask the jellyfish
how the
Kelp flow with grace so easily. The jellyfish sizzled 'round
my
Neck, heaving, "Acknowledge what sinks down and
Erupts out of here. Once you realize how
Simple the answer is, you will not only glide like the kelp
but also
Sing aloud the siren resting comatose in you."

In This Dopey Room

JANUARY 14, 2018

I thought of Tori Amos's song 'iieee' as I wrote this and, well, my nerves go through the roof whenever I must sing in a karaoke room, as I've always been judged for my weak singing voice.

Hummm mmmm
You take your hands off my eyes and we're in a smoky room.
Normally, the sight of nicotine bodies wavering in and out of consciousness
rings unattractive to me,
but today, I'm with you in this dopey room.
My surging blood can relax a little.

Hyuuuuu nnnnn
It's not merely cancer floating in zero gravity.
The lightning suns are flickering,
bickering in inaudible sign language.
Are we actors in a horror film?
I think they're just setting the mood.

Hwaaaa ahhhh haaa
The telly-screen shoots sparks and they belly dance on the tables.
The residents of the metallic box threaten to call the police on us.
They scrape off guitar strings, throw up their larynxes,
and their bloated drums signal the thunder.
White letters poke through their hypnotic rave, and yellow rays trickle into the words.

Heeeeeee
You hand me a microphone.
Right before this moment you were belting the keys of

your mama's piano.
I swear a halo swung about above you.
Now, I'm back in this dopey room. Get that stick away from me.
You're fully aware that my chords are chronically ill.

o
This is the prime time,
the purpose of our stay.
Eyes write down the empty words,
but they don't translate where I taste.

I want this smoke to hallucinate
along with your musical waves,
but no higher power can confiscate
the adrenaline reigning this haze.
You rub my spine with urgent care
as if it were still cartilage.
Your face magnetizes to this mic
and your voice detects what's wrong with it.

ahaaaaaahaaaa
The mic streams your song to my ears.
Suddenly, my own could not resist.
So, we sang into this robotic stick, together,
in this room of dopey mist.

In A Dream That Couldn't Be

JANUARY 19, 2018

An acrostic for Tori Amos, which includes lyrics from 'Winter'.

My second mother, though we aren't linked through umbilical cords or DNA curls,
Yodels soprano symphonies that pluck my meatiest string of har(p) (t).
Rain showers through her red velvet tresses and ride my cotton swirls
As she tip-taps the millionth black-white key from Mars.

Eve of a straining day, my brain plays a disturbing tape. There you are,
Light, almost life-like, gazing behind my own piano performance. My under eyes are
Lead-filled, swollen from ocean spray, as I play my grave song. News told me you would
Eventually leave, as we all do, but this movie, like an impatient child, sped to the end too soon!
Now I sit here so pitiful and lame, deceived by chemical fiction. (Yeah, I'm gullible. I admit it.)

A crack in my voice leaps out. I can't handle this anymore, so I flee to your embrace.
Miserable fire trucks speed with no regard for traffic, all down my face and to your chest.
"**O**h— It can't be you! Is it you? Raisin mommy, why did you have to leave me, too?!"
Spit. Blood. Carbon air. Came out of me, but not from you. My nails stab your gelatin back.

(,)

Is this the last I'll see of you?

Last... last... no... You were my final push for life, mother...
On the forty-fifth ticking minute, your Styrofoam fingers stroke my yarn ball mane and your
Voice slows down my thrashing veins: *When you gonna love you as much as I do?...*
End scene. That's when it all faded to black.

Yelling in my head, I scramble to my phone and I search up her name.
On the screen which blinds white, there is no mention of her death day.
Unimaginably relieved, yet I don't believe it for a while.
Though, I must have faith in something.

She is the Torrey pine blocking the ultraviolet rays.
Odd mother, she never was mine. (In *my soul* she is permanently engraved.)

Rainbow Hill

January 20, 2018

I have a confession to spill.
I'm afraid I fell off that rainbow hill
a long, awfully long time ago.
I'm petrified of the ghost
that seems to be telling you lies
of the life that I live unwise.

I'm astonished I'm not strapped to metal yet;
my fingers still hook on the edge of that battle nest.
Oh! when I introduce myself to the sun again
she only seems to take. No, she never lends.

She steals my hours of much needed rest
and replaces it with Satan's words filling up my chest.
She loots my ability to hear crystal clear
and gives me looks of confusion from folks and my peers.
She sucks out all trace of my guide serotonin
and leaves me with vision two-colored and homeless.

I confess I've forgotten how people react
when they mourn for a dog but not for a calf.
I confess that my knowledge of being is wiped;
I could see your seasoned tears and not feel contrite.
I also confess that this is slight exaggeration,
But someday, they'll shoot down my door and all will
come to fruition.

I want to wince from puffed cuts the same way you do,
but I confess... I'm far spaced from your ways and I'm
through.

The Skin Bleach Lotion

FEBRUARY 1?, 2018

"Take it. Put it on."
I refused.
"Why not?"

"Because why should I crawl up slippery stairs to the asymptotic standard?

Why would I smolder this cast
which loves me unconditionally?

This blanket which hugs my organs so intimately that even my prudish heart kisses back furiously?

This veil that rushes my cells when a cut bleeds, or whispers my head to sleep?
Or dies trying to sustain me?

This binding defines true motherly love. It does not care about the visual— only the essential. It exceeds the love you'd find from anyone, really. And I don't think that's quite gotten to you, yet."

I perused the ingredient list.
"If I douse myself with this, then I don't love anything."

Pick Up Your Phone...

FEBRUARY 2, 2018

Open your petals. You can trust me.
Look up.
Nailed to the concrete is the neon heading:
CALL
Not 911. (Unless you need to.)
Read the lucent lettering.
Let its remnants linger in your vision a little longer.
Call out.
Pray. Attract. Or simply whisper a mantra:

「I am safe up here in outer space.
No black hole, no matter how hungry, can siphon me.
I bear magic— I uphold the power to change. 」

When skyscrapers are up in flames and the horizon is
Hell's gates:

Call.
Someone will answer.

Do You Know Where My Mother Is?

FEBRUARY 8?, 2018

Here I am, without my mother.

I.

This fire makes a decent substitute, but she isn't here to stay. A booming blow to her head is enough for it to flake to black ash. Somehow, it is a deeper hue than the stagnant sky.

II.

In the daytime, you can distinguish an eleven-morning sun from a three-afternoon sun, but in the night: it's the same
unlit room, and the sky's flashlight does not come nor go, not even if a fever has struck the poor young soul. A concept so permanent? So impossible. Without our mother's embrace, we will succumb to drip dropping icicles and freeze in the night's eyes.

III.

All I hear is crackling. All I see are sparks. All my nose detects is melting wood and they beg in my ears for mercy: "I'm dying! Oh Lord, I don't wanna go!" That's too bad. Your begging only gives me tingles, popping around my skull. So, I dare you, scream a little louder, so ringing that you will hear my head, too.

IV.

I called to the wind, but the message drifted farther from the destination. A journey, one may think to call it. I thought I held the paper scissors to cut off any forks in the road. On the other side of the mountains, I was a plane pilot: breezed through the night sky with no inkling of fright... I want so badly to soar once more, but the mountains stand so great and glorious before me...

Impact

FEBRUARY 12?, 2018

The smallest opposing ripple
can subdue the crash of
an island's high tide.

Severed Ropes

FEBRUARY 15, 2018

The root cause of our severed ropes,
our obsidian walls,
and the glass on the floor
is our *unrepentant selfishness*, which when fully
provoked, reeks through our eyes, our nose,
and the most despicable path: our throats.

Romanticizing

FEBRUARY 28, 2018

There is nothing romantic about a lone wolf
who trudges through sugar reeds and poison ivy
to pinpoint where the path split in two.
No trace of beauty exists in the liquid pleading
which crawls and shoves through her matted fur.

What is romantic about her howls?
Absolutely nothing.
The demented will twist it to sound like the smooth river down south,
but it mirrors the slashing tides of the river right of us.
They are not howls of triumph, nor celebration;
they are howls clutching for a stone, for the next low tide before the waterfall.

She is growling, moaning, foaming at the mouth.
The effort is wasteful — it's pointless — for her pack has fled the scene already.
They won't return
because the lone wolf carries scalding bolts that the others fear to contact.
Or never tried to touch.

Ah, again.
Roaming through groans, foam slops the ground:

I'm so lonely... Can anybody hear me?
I'm shrieking, bursting my organs inside!
Somebody, please give me a reason to feel
that I'm needed or loved or I'm already near!
Near your fire, your lumber; or you, a liar.

I don't want to be here, all alone alone alone—
No more! Not anymore! Drag me with you!

Yet (and they told me this time and time again),
No one is coming to save me (unless He is daring).
As the pack's already sped south
where the river bends with ease and the moon flutters
eyes at her reflection.
I will spin in circles, blind from the compass.
My brain drunk, I may eventually stagger into the
eastward river and sink to the pit. (Only time will tell.)

How can you find it breathtaking when bubbles no longer
tap the surface?

A Sphere So Abundant and Round

MARCH 1?, 2018

I.

I live in a sphere so abundant and round.
Oft I wish my limbs could embrace this mound
and show her my appreciation for my chance to be.

II.

No road is completely smooth.
Life was drawn like this, intentionally.
Intentionally.
Every road has cracks and ditches, weathered by
hurricanes and the like.
I must remind myself of this, even when a thing called
envy controls me.

The Pendulum

MARCH 3, 2018

The pendulum swings rightward,
leftward.
Never a decimal too little or much
in the distance it travels.

The dilated pupils dart rightward,
leftward,
mimicking this curious apparatus,
if we could call it such.

The weeks swindle rightward,
leftward,
wherein one day, traffic flows like a stream
and in another, the pelican paralyzes in winds.

I reach rightward,
leftward,
to find which product will fulfill me best
and keep my gluttony satiated and fed.

My words shuffle rightward,
leftward.
Copying the pendulum,
contradicting my ways.

Pupils hypnotize rightward,
leftward,
and cannot crawl out of this maze.

The pendulum is only obeying physics' laws,
but it is not healthful for a body to mirror the actions
of a pendulum
as all battery will run out
and pleading guilty will not save you.

Why I Need the Sand

MARCH 7?, 2018

I want it all to end with a close of a lid,
a dream to float me above cooling seas:
where the sky is never silver and it's never cold, constant gold—
where I know this home will never wither.

As I write this, tears clutch my eyes;
when I blink, I let them soar with gravity's shove.
I want them to sing that spring song and face the real
horror of evaporating, not kissing the ground.
Yet, next up is their kingdom come.
Life is so beautiful. Not every womb gets to touch its
parts. I am so thankful! Know I am grateful!

Yet, such beauty is too harsh on the eyes at times.
With every passing day, my sanity sails farther away.
Reality mixes in my sleep.
Is this horror? Is this fantasy?
Apathy is the island queen. I can feel her magma
rumbling in me, smacking smog to my clarity.
When?
Will I erupt? I pray, someone hear me, my volcanic
engine remains inactive!

The only thing that keeps me from chugging all the
ocean, or whatever insanity sparks me,
are the words engraved here in white sand.
The only property where my blood baths can run and not
drench me, at least for a few minutes.
It isn't always print or quite Orthodox,
and the blue waves may scrub this history away,
but I know its once place, so I think it will be okay.

I am not sorry for this brown, gritty beach,
because then I'd be sorry for the air that I breathe.

To Be A Body

March 9, 2018

'Tis a fiery winter day.
Yet the sun could not come on time,
so she smeared lead above our heads,
letting us know she could not step out of her room.
If you simply look out a tear-stained window,
you could not tell she was lugging damp tissues in her sockets.

I traverse through her humid arteries,
but oft I do so; yeah, I'm used to it.
It's the package deal for sharing this space.
I traverse without power over my own two feet.
How fascinating: I'm cutting ties with my own body!

Yonderly, my toes inch forward and closer
to the green palms at the edge.
Torsos sway, sessile giants: these alcoholic trees,
always drunk when they should not be.
Intoxication never took me, but my body mirrors their dancing lean.

My neck bends behind and the sun's blood sprays me.
Colored in salt-licked Oceania, it houses other family members.
Wooing my body to rent a room in it.

The palms, or the sea?
What shall it be?
It wouldn't matter to her as I'm only one of many in her system,
and I'm only one of few on this cell.
To be frank, no one else would notice, and they would not bother searching.
We are introverted creatures in the sun's womb;
we all need a view of her light, too.

Breakfast with Heaven

MARCH 11?, 2018

I'm instilled with addictions to pixel screens.
My eyes cannot split this strange creature clearly.
At times all I know is reality's bliss
Is solely this true-to-life vain canvas.

And yet, I'll wake to the dawn on my left
To capture her vintage good morning message.
The cursive pops with vanilla-esque tuft
And behind it, she irons the azureish brush.

Birds wheeze with glee when golden brown drifts
Across their feathers and their brood dragon eggs.
And I react the same
When nature pours honey stripes down on my face.

When my children shall see their first risen sun,
I hope that the image of Heaven light stays.
For indulging machinery's fine in bite-size,
But breakfast with Heaven is nutrient baked!

The Most Admirable Trait

MARCH 12?, 2018

While lying on the hospital bed,
you spot the dust mite.
He hides his face behind plastic curtains.
Three simple words trail out your breath:
“I forgive you.”

Simple from simpleton view, but try wrapping ten fingers
‘round an olive branch, holding
it to the yellow dot in the sky. If your eyelids tempt
to seal then your word is not the truth.

To thank for the past and move past...
Mm, only a swollen tongue and chamber can flex a
weight so drab.

To embrace without hate is the most admirable action
one can do!
It shall do good, I promise you.

Progression

MARCH 15?, 2018

We would all be better off
with our mouths sewn closed.

Even better:
with our mind's voice muted or low.

And best:
listening without a single groan.

Higher

I.

(MARCH 17, 2018)

How whimsical to realize
that the universe is, at first glance,
nothing at all,
but simultaneously
everything we know and don't?
It is intangible. It is incomprehensible to the human psyche.

Maybe it really is just fiction.

Yet, there is that slight off chance that it saturates every meter of our being,
our environment, inanimate or living.
This ghostly machinery,
however cruel or magnanimous,
maps out our courses and ties knots where it must.

To debate coincidence or fate is beyond us, for could we ever really know so?
Even when we rest in peace, will we see it then?
Will we ever know? Should we ever know...

II.

(JANUARY 22, 2019)

Fret not: in the grounds, I'm embedded in this concinnity.
I rest upon this assertion. Fragile heart, quiver not!
These are plain laws. Experimentation won't please,
but even cataracts slide out my pupils. I expose my
vessel,
I trust the routine:
The sun rises, the clouds glide, the night is ebony!

I am the concinnity
but born from myself?
I won't falsely claim.
I will say: patterns are set.
I trust the routine.

With my tremulous fingers, the cloud buster guides me:
make days come from rainfall to sun fall;
uncover the double entendre.

*magnanimous – generous, high-minded
*concinnity – harmonious arrangement (God, in this context)
*cloud buster – device that turns energy in the atmosphere to rain
*double entendre – ambiguity; multiple meanings

Autumn Tundra All Around

MARCH 23?, 2018

An autumn tundra all around.
I do not hear a hush or shout.
I try to feel the drums of chest,
but hands are pasted on cement.
The outstretched jungle stands behind.
Trees cross their vines and smirk all while
I slip the pond some ways ahead.
The vultures swarm me; am I dead?

One tries to nick my shoulder rock.
Somehow, I knock her beak and claw.
I call, recall; I am a hooved
pony: horned, and satin-looked.
This world is solely tundra grass.
Parched ground but sop, this no man's land.
My hooves pulse on and on and on
to notes of syringe dots unlocked.

Comes home the thunderous, proud Parent
who slams into the grass mattress.
Sweat from overtime spritzes on me.
I do not cringe; instead, I sneeze.
Then there I feel a stillness thump
Against my eyes and near my lungs
My bass of heart is ringing clear!
I did not need my hand to feel.

I had to revert to a womb
and drink the wilderness's rain.
Labor does circumnavigate;
I needed the proof and proof I got.
My hooves, in fact, mimic the bass
produced in the heart and in the plains.

Colorful Ones

MARCH 25?, 2018

I am not an ugly color.
"Ugly" cannot apply to this!
I am just a hue on the spectrum;
though, aren't we all?
This greenhouse carries a rainbow...
Isn't that so marvelous?

Concertina

MARCH 27, 2018

The four zeroes are glowing, the neon white not gentle.
My mind has disconnected—
I must trudge through this, Concertina style.
Be the gun, I say, pull the trigger.
Don't bite the bullet— become a bullet shower!

Remaining coiled is one option,
And maybe the favorable position,
But even in time the metal will rust
So either way, there is no visit from luck.
Comfort is there, yes, but sanity?
I am no vain constrictor. Ugly reaches vanity.

This mercury boil could pinch me,
But it won't expose a bone.
Burn, you can try and test me,
But the laws abide, you're overthrown.

I don't always need the infinity of numbers
To lull a 'bye!' on my nightly mile.
Sometimes we need to shut the blinds,
And approach this, Concertina style.
Be the gun, be the finger pulling that trigger.
Don't bite the bullet— become a bullet shower!

Pleaser

April 5, 2018

She ridiculed me for licking the honey sapped on the page.
She cannot look at me, small pupil to large pupil, because I wait for tingles on my skin.

She shoved me down to the tiled floor because I wanted to embrace.
She thought of me *irritating irritating god why does she follow me everywhere little devil when is she gonna attack*

and now my spine curls ever more to the elderly stature.
now you're undesirable who wants an adult who laughs like a child but slumps like a dead willow my god so ***annoying***

My arms wrap around myself now... I don't remember a time, after that time, when I openly embraced with my heart beating against another like tendon. *go away you seriously need to*

What would I give to hug her again? What could I do to preserve her free spirit? I don't know... *grow up and stop being selfish*

I'm told this is what time does to you: *listen carefully since you only listen to yourself*
Heal? Maybe the scar is still tender. The skin is still sunburnt.

I don't need you anymore.

I still love you.

The Pearl in Pansies

APRIL 14, 2018

Perhaps I read my first Sylvia Plath poem around this point, inspiring this piece. This is an ambiguous poem about how the school system does not properly prepare students to succeed in the adult world, yet the adult world punishes us for living through life blindly. As aforementioned, this is a highly ambiguous poem, so I oblige you to form your own interpretation.

The crowd is laughing at me. Why aren't they stopping?
Tricked, I thought the ticket would show me
the pearl in the pansy.

To avert, my eyes wish on me.
One quarter from seats, but wholly
from the bittersweet memory:
Final product on the manipulated
sheet. How it itches; it's etched on me.

Like the gold vacuumed
From the house fire.
Methane gas huffed out the rabbit hole.
Coal grass blanketed it,
obviously.
A mere nugget can't save everything.
We know this already.

Atolls raged out my dermis,
but was it from the sulfuric rain,
or this fog of dry ice?

Spring sets on us palm sisters,
but winter withers white way up there.

No blizzard here.
Perfect, yes perfect!
The flowers must wash ashore.

I nourished them, wept them, left them
all to the clouds
who slept them, fed them, wed them
to the dirt stripped of fertilizer.

Golden never licked the seed.
Not my fault, not my problem.
A grain of sand will march in eventually,
It just takes time, they need some patience.
Develop some grit, eat potassium from the air, get it there.

Wait, a decade has subtracted already?
The years were a plus for them!
Where's the purple? The yellow?
The green?
The pearl!

The pot moved a floor above.
And behold, the next day
I saw one vermillion torso,
beheaded, but almost
whole, almost more so.
Both wings intact, the
solitude
enough to rise out this cobwebbing dirt.
Have grit, babe. Keep on.

Then the night came.
The somber light glitched on me.
I came home to the pot
with a black lake.
—But only that.

Black lake, what did you do to my
creation, my neo-tradition!
Did you let a crow eat? Did the wind cage the weed?
Well fine!
I'll shoot that crow in the eye.
I'll swallow the breeze so that it will hurl
my one prosperity.

I demand in my palms: the pearl in pansies!

Embrace & Evolve

MAY 3, 2018

After watching Unreported World's video covering an acid attack survivor daily life, I cried furious tears. I knew I had to write about it.

Power and control.
Those two, your favorite words;
I'm not allowed one.

"Dig holes to China."
Priests tell me that's how you do.
No "I do's" from you.

And you never say,
But I have that right as well!
You bull, seeing red.

My coils fray in
Carolina Reaper soup.
My skin's curdling, too!

Then you flee— you're free.
My body boils down to
Gum on some sidewalk.

A scraper saves me.
Whose hand, I can't say surely.
But now I'm home safe.

Acid burn, pond murk;
It can never be bedtime.
Now it's just bath time.

This bath's like lava,
But I've felt real Venus rain
Roast me inside-out.

I wish my bare skin
Would weld onto this bound'ry
But I've acid in me.

Did you know, my Lo,
That suds don't stain nor glisten?
Sulfate purloins stares.

But swelled skin steals glares.
My knees surface... poke circles.
Water's now mirror.

Serial Killer—
The monstrous undead's unleashed!
Loved ones run from me!

Acid burn, pond murk;
(My eyes try twitching from grip.)
The two comprise me.

but
I don't want to prune
And shrink to two unlike things.
For I, I'm Lita.
You're neither Lo or Lita.
I'll reclaim your proudest words:

Power to embrace;
Control to evolve.
Embrace the water; evolve
Past your banal sin nature.

The Believers? They Stay.

May 7?, 2018

I'm sorry. This is reality.
Reliance on a Beam beyond the sky will stay.
I'm sorry to tell you: it may always be this way.
I know, we have fingers to point a check from an x
Without some pixie glue to piece each joint together.
Just look at me. I am like you, no doubt.

Maybe you will never want to see holes shaved
Out the clouds.
But you and I must learn to accept that
Some people, who are like me and you, beg to see those
Particles cast unto by chartreuse.
Those children have nothing else to hope for.

The binary codes, algebraic tolls
Do not hum any sort of symphony
To the average person, at least not to the brim of their
Coal-colored, grim toils.
Call them delusional, brand them dreamers,
But for much of the world, they bathe in "believer."

I'm condemned for believing, I'm condemned for not.
This senseless tug-of-war, and all for what?

Ridiculing the Knot of Beauty

May 10?, 2018

For those who say, “Poetry should be obsolete.”

I will laugh in your face. If poetry should go extinct, then
that means we’ve done it.
We’ve seen the Universe in a bodily, digestible form and
we’ve slaughtered it. No more babies are on their
deathbeds from malnutrition. People everywhere are
treated as equals. No more tears are leaving.
But all of this happens a millisecond before the Earth
combusts. You will not get to enjoy a poetry-less world
for one whole moment.

We cannot rebel against this knot of beauty.

What Will Go Lost

JUNE 8, 2018

No life covers you.
You wouldn't like to admit this:
but by default you think life submits
to your orders, your rules.

Already, the Gilded Sky hears all complaints—
why do you think we are at war every day?

Bend down to me! You're mine to please!
Today, I'd like sun rays to overlay.

The high blue rolls its wispy tongue
condensed with saliva to bruise a black lung.
It spits and hollers and coughs on your back,
till the standing ovation: bolts leaving ash where it
jabbed.

Be quiet, then: you mustn't speak.
Observe what was lost and will go lost.
Then see what the rain has made, not taken.
The playground's far from reach, but to submerge wholly
in the puddles surrounding
heeds the necessary.

The end all: Unattainable is never physical.
It is our inexcusable mental bulwark.
This is what pulls us away from the hilltop and closer
to greed.

I Can't Hand You

JUNE 9, 2018

Do you love me?
From top to knee,
and feet to throat,
oh, love, would you?

I fidget with my buttons
and sow my cotton seed hair.
I know that breath exiting your insides:
the sigh, the brutal no-nod
wringing your neck all bloodless.

Do I love the clam, still,
when it could never house
a pearl: oily, ridgeless?

Oh— no, I think not. So why should you?

You who nodded yes:
I deny to hear you say a why.
Since I... I
have received plenty during my time.
This candy sweet only chokes me.
I have no nacre to numb me.
I am a clam with gummy meat,
Alas! no pearl to rip from me.
I may have had one, may have not.
So don't come ask me where it's gone.

I cannot even give you baroque.

I'm sorry.

I know you well, poor farmer.

So sorry.

You will dump me back to seawater.

I'm useless.

And someone else will boot the cycle.

I swear I will be better then.

Don't tell me the ocean won't crash me on rocks.
That is its purpose: to mesh me with the smog.

Void

JUNE 9, 2018

I have come to the conclusion
that this suppression, this nothingness,
fills me with utmost content.

「Are these not the last words of the sane? 」

The Logical End

AUGUST 28, 2018

On the night before my first day of my senior year of high school, my parents were (quite audibly) distressed from solving how to finance my schooling. They were already in deep debt, so I felt like a burden.

Gone.
A sweet, then salty, pattern.
Gone should describe the me of tomorrow.
Off where, I cannot think.
I'll either be feared into that melting hole,
or somewhere... but not really there.

Death shall part me from all I have known.
My squirming side aches for the grand scope.
Ins and outs and ups and...

Gone is my unerring adjective.
My have been, is, will be.
Gone is what I should be.
So, Death, pull me into the eye.
I can dance with the dark or the light.

For my mother dreads the envelope, Death.
She knows only dust fits inside it.
These metal birds terrify my poor father;
He must stretch to both poles to profit.

I'm already a full empty vase.
You may as well drop me.
You know this is the logical end.

Amending the VI

NOVEMBER 22, 2018

Four score and seven years have passed.
For some reason, I'm here, amidst the last stand.

Frustrated, I am;
Dishonest, I am not.
You are not the law, little girl.

Muscle contracts in your center,
But no blood flies out!
You haunted, two-faced little girl.

Proper prose
to no avail on your palate, black rose.
You try and shout obscenities...
But nobody on Earth is listening!

You drool syrup from your teeth.
It sputters and strings as you squeal your writhing.
The lone fool you are: you think you are funny.
Yet, oh wow, you are the only one laughing!

Repudiate all you can,
The canine gem's still dead.
Oh! I forget—
You mauled his body to the grave.

Inside your mass, a verdant spirit festers,
But I am on the floor, in tears and dying to ask:
"Are you not jaded? Would it not be better
To slash and hurl this burden you rack?

You turn the other way.
Away from fate, away from right history.

Lost Sheep

NOVEMBER 24, 2018

In which I officially come to Christ.

I deplore Him
for these happenings!
O despise my fervent, volatile spirit, Lord.
I drown myself in the depths of the Mariana's trench.
All for nothing!

Why have I been dragged into this asylum?
Why could not have I been just one dust atom?
To dissolve into air would have given me
Lust.
Of this, I am much aware.

I stitch these words onto this frame,
Yet, I still feel all the same.
I beg that Someone harbor these
Atrocious thoughts that choke my teeth.

For friends I have— and yet I don't
(As I do thrive in distance).
You nurse me full; I'm far from You.
Kindle the twigs! Spark up my soul!

I am an empty solid.
I do know what "fixed" is
In particles, not nature.
I ache for fluidity. I am absent-minded of feeling.
To be miles more than just matter...
I long for the day, my dearest Father.

MY FIRST LOVE: MY SALVE & MY SECONDMOST SIGNIFICANT ABANDONER | 2019

AGES 17 & 18

I THOUGHT GOD GIFTED ME MY BRIGHTEST BLESSING. AFTER YEARS OF TURNED HEADS, I THOUGHT YOU WOULD BE THE ONE TO LATCH. NO. GOD RIPPED YOU AWAY, TOO. ADHESION WASN'T YOUR BIRTHRIGHT IN THE FIRST PLACE.

MEXICAN
PEGASUS
BOY
GENERAL

To Search for You, God in the Flesh

I.

(APRIL 3, 2019)

To search for God in the flesh
is a mistake; thus, ensue the magma:
ravish bones whole, and the spirit dissipates.

To search for permanence in the already rotten
will thrust you unprepared.

I tried to find a God in you.
'Twas accidental. I swear.
You took me in with dead winter surrounding us.
I fell for it. I am in a pit.

I am left worse than I started off.
I would love to blame it on you, but that is child's play.

Who, in the flesh, do I trust? Who must I settle for?

II.

(JANUARY 6, 2020)

To think that the Almighty trusted you with me puzzles me so.
You belong in the center of it all.

You — a blessing that has enriched my fibrous being — were,
too, the chastisement I hadn't a clue I needed to remunerate for.

In debt I was, but what for?
In debt of that— my fibrous being!

I reside in a shelter that is withering, though stable.
Winter smacks the outer walls, but I am warmer.
The floor creaks and a part of something still attached to me tatters underneath my bare feet.
I fear for my life: that the toasty indoors will rip from the mud,
and that the pit is near and awaits me.

Perhaps I shall tumble right back.
A sliver of me, indifferent, invites this day.
The larger piece, hidden beneath the foundation, refuses to open the door.

I am aware if I choose to run, it will suck me in. Not if, but when?
Brace yourself. (Life is what made this.)

Lysso

APRIL 18, 2019

I clutch the noose, and I wear it like a crown. It pricks my scalp, as years of neglect had left the rope's circumference all frayed and sharp. Heavy, too. My eyes shut gently, and I stand on my toes. I am weightless, for if I believe it to be, I am; or at least I've been told so.

I am not the noise; I am a single strand, unwavering against the odds. No crossings nor snaps: just a flatline across the heart meter.

I summon a strange thing. Strange, but by no means a stranger.

In all the frankness I can claw at, and gather in my nails—
in all the ingenuity, at its core definition, that I can muster,
I am terrified, still.

Lysso,
will you save me? Will you drive my body asunder for the rest of my days?

*Lysso- derived from lyssophobia: the fear of going insane (phobia – fear; lysso – insanity)

My Letter (to You)

APRIL 23, 2019

The letter I never had the chance to hand You.

April. Twenty-third. Twenty nineteen.
Procrastination has had me offset.
I meant to write this long before now.
Yet, God has his ways... my mind was frazzled then...
Still is. Though now I see more similar edges to connect to.

So here it goes...

And all the names I give you.

Writing usually comes easily to me.
For a reason unbeknownst to me, my fingers now can't find the keys.
Perhaps it's the lack of sleep you've given me.

Between us, no borders lie.
So, allow me:
I love you. Thank you. Thank you so much.
If not for you, where would I be?

Sorry, let's address the "I love you."

Yes, my heart once pounced at the thought of you.
I thought you would have been my first love.
I thought you would have been my first kiss.
I thought you would have been the first I would have shared many romantic moments with.

I thought you would be the first of many things.
No, but in other ways yes.
You were the first person I could express myself freely to in two years.
You were the first to listen to my ramblings.

You are the first boy that my nerves did not shudder around.
You are my first guy friend.
You were the first boy to express your vulnerabilities to me.
You were the first boy to hold my hand when I needed support.
You were the first person that I cried for
out of immense gratitude.

I love you. I do.
Love, you know, has many definitions.
You maybe were thinking I still crush on you.
I do not lust for you. What I feel is much more expansive.
Which is why when you rejected me, I did not leave you.

In simple words: my life has changed because of you.
You think you do not do much for me.
From the outside that's true.
What matters here, though, is my inside.
Inside, the butterfly crawled out of its cocoon.
Because of you, now I know:
There was never anything wrong with me.
I deserve the love that I receive.

Yeah, maybe the people I wanted most did not want me,
but that doesn't mean nobody wanted me.
I needed to outsource my love.

You think your loved ones hate you.
Well, I am one 'loved one'.
And I don't hate you.

You think they all want out because there's something about you.
But the reason I want *in* is that something in you.
You are important, ███. Please know that and wear that fact proudly.
I repeat, if not for you, I don't know where I would be.

You harbor much tough love in you. I was always understanding of that.
In fact, your tough love was what ushered me into metamorphosis.
"You have to make the change."
Not verbatim, but something like that.
Look, ███! I made the change!

Are you proud of me?

Ugh, I hate my dependency: I told myself that if you forget me
I would be indifferent because your mark has already done so much.
Yet every time I say this, a flood rushes out of me.
(Oops, I am quite the mess in my spare time.)
I am not very sure what I am to you:
Some girl who worked with your friends,
or
a friend who means a lot to you.

Do you believe in soulmates, ███?
I believe that humans can have more than one.
You are a soulmate.

You laugh at the idea of God.
Which is fine. I could care less.
Maybe you'll laugh at what I write next:
You are proof that God exists.
He knew I needed to flourish to survive.
So then *plop!* You arrived.
The night I first met you, I knew right away you changed something in me.
I didn't know what exactly then, but now I know:

I sheltered myself before. Now I grab at any possible opportunity! I talk to more people!

This part is most difficult: reciprocity.
I am probably nothing to you.

Should I walk away before this hurts more than necessary?
If I do, then is this proof that all my efforts in anyone I choose is a waste?

Must I march back to my dreamworld
where only I control my fate?

The Tickle of a Wall

APRIL 25, 2019

I hate the tickle of a wall against my skin.
Even more so when on the other side, fattened pupils
haze me.
I hate all forms of extremity:

The skin burns that the Sun
brands during a midsummer month,
or the same injury designed from
frost bitten blizzard cold.

I've discovered a nasty code:
We hide a sadist under our clothes.

So, while I quote myself,
"I hate all forms of extremity."
I cannot retract and replace:
"I dislike all forms of extrem—" No.
You know what I said; it's in the air.
We hide a sadist under our clothes.

An Innervation Ineffable

APRIL 25, 2019

I.

My love for you all is ever flowing...
I think I know the reason why.
I desire that reciprocation.
I know. It will never come.

I should leave it at that,
but I can't for reasons unbeknownst to me.
One day, I will reach my breaking point.

I will leave. None of you will care much.
The shock of the news will travel through you like the wind of a hurricane.

Then the sun will follow in the pink.
Back to the norm of daily life.

II.

The irony has weakened my knees!
My arms reach more lips,
yet I feel even more alone.

The risk is higher...
More chances of connection,
even more of failure.

They will all abandon me.
I trust the repeatability of science.
I trust that the continuation will flow.

If you see that I care, you will hiss.
So, I'll attend to you only for a bit.
If I tarry for a minute too much,
I will be shoved deeper than the start.

Christ loves me unconditionally.
The rest of this is a blink.
You will vanish.
He won't.

So, Heaven, I call for you on the spot:
If I choose my own time to flee,
will you punish me?
You are so understanding!

You understand all well that
sin is rampant inside me:
greedy and selfish describes me.
But is it greedy to ravish my glee?
I can't stand the octave climbing.
Let it drop so I can get it over with.

Oh, how packed the world is full of inauthenticity.
So much white noise.
Is it so selfish to want to see green?
The forest, the mountains... where it's just me?

Small talk is lust.
If I hit you with the hard truth you run. This happens, always.
I never want to be a bother. That is why I lay in bed so much.
The only bother I can be is one to myself.

III.

I fear being too extreme.
Nobody likes a girl
who bawls herself to sleep because she doesn't know the appropriate hours
of when to let the drops tap, not flood.
I have it all come out at once.

IV.

I think I am the master of deception:
I seem quiet and pure, but I can be flamboyant and cocky.
People seem to flock to me, but once I show them the sweet spot they turn away.

Life seems dandy to them, but they don't know that I can never seem to stop crying.
I cry during my meals alone. Then I'll sing some. Then immediately cry some more.

I get too excited at the thought that someone would listen.
No. Family leaves. Friends leave. They all forget too.

God, I beg! Let me leave!

I know I promised him I wouldn't act this way, but he does not care for me!
I know it... and I pretend to be fine about it because that is how I cope.
I know the slashings will only continue, so why hurt myself more?
When it could just end in a split second?

Nirai Lady

MAY 2, 2019

An acrostic for my mother.

Nirai Lady, whose dagger bounces off,
Emerges from the Himalayan silk floor.
Vapor mists out her neck, rising towards
Eden, the kingdom on the mountain top,
Reaching for the first sunrise touch.

Winter guts her the higher up.
Amidst the meal's finale, nothing is felt.
She digested a satellite's note; it ripples, not missing a single detail:

'**W**hy?' She suppressed that vital thought until now.
Elevation does not defer from looking below.
Ah, I am still and tranquil.
Kilometers of climbing are not needed.

*nirai – Japanese for 'heaven'

WHAT APPEARS ONCE I LOOK DOWN

MAY 2, 2019

Present, yet wholly decomposed;
alone, yet girthing me was a buzz! It walled me in!
I was sure the Invisibility, haunted, was taunting me.

I'm plopped a tad higher: all was necessary.
I'm still a present shadow in my own island,
though now my tide emerges:

I observe that the ebb had shed from us both.
All along, the Intangible adorned you with these details,
too.

To You, the Cherub

JUNE 30, 2019

In which I use a clogyrnach, a haiku, a somonka, a quatrain, a tanka, and a free verse poem.

The night! The night has no limit.
The blood moon oozes iron fill.
I am no stranger.
Just came now, later.
This false divulgence.

My mouth pops open.
Thus, all my vessels close shut.
I am real no more:

I called out to you!
The cherub, who comes and goes
Whenever he pleases.
The red string wraps 'round your waist.
I tug it, whilst bawling in mute.

Call? But I am deaf.
Only blood, the moon, is red.
There's a place beneath
For hollow things like yourself.
A holy being? I am not.

Just as he says, he is not one.
Never ever will he come close.
See, habitually I worship
Falsely, then I'm showered with hope.

Jubilantly, I gulp it all.
The water fills in me, making
Sure the buoyancy can hold
A foundation... a kingdom.

Jelly. It was only jelly.
The jelly engulfs the rough draft.
It slid out. Excavation through.
Now again! Again! My skin's loose.

Janitor — you'll do — clean this up!
I shall not leave till I flatten.
You winged sadist, I am full
Of blood! And of all you beasts.

I declare it so.
Past you, the Sky spoke clearly:
"Don't fray the design
of cherubs, who'll print lip stains
and flee far, to start from scratch.

Cherubs die during their construction. I am eternal.
Come to me, only I can love you.
Only in me will a kingdom come."

The Sixth of December, 2019

DECEMBER 8, 2019

Written days after subsequently living through the Pensacola Naval Air Station shooting/terrorist attack.

Black.
I could not hear a breath. Breaths were not allowed.
I looked onward. Nothing hypothetical, only the literal.
What was seen forward? Black.
And I felt nothing.
My mouth was dry, my legs stiff.
"These are my last seconds alive. When will I die?"
If you had rushed in, 'now' was the optimal time.

Time of death: around 8 AM on some day in December 2019.

For if you had, I knew damn well I would not have struck you. Or even ran or hid. No will sustained in me.
I questioned many things:

I.

Why did I stop praying to God? As if I only needed him in dire moments such as this?

My God is the utmost of the utmost. And though He's quite aware of this, he opts to humble himself. He could punish me for forgetting him, but he never forgot me:

He spared me from hearing pops from a gun.
The ones whom the bullets caught.
The bad man rotting in his own blood on the road.
Screams of frightened witnesses.

I get to live a little longer because the bad man was in a different place. (I pray those who died traveled safely to the afterlife.)

II.

Am I good enough?
I entered my new life blind. I underestimated the standards that are placed.
"You're too weak." "How did you get here?"
"You could die on the battlefield, you know! See heads explode in front of you."

"You're not good enough."

I never heard much of those statements until now. Man, do they sting deep.

I couldn't handle just the thought of seeing ONE man pointing a gun in my face. How would I manage seeing dozens and more doing the same?
Once I opened up about this, sneers and rolling eyes met me.

Why am I here... why am I here... why am I here...

III.

I thought I was safe here.

Though doubts attacked me along this journey — at first from others then they sourced from myself — I settled down at a moment's notice. I observed it was necessary. If I didn't, I would be an outsider.

A rushing heart ALL the time is abnormal, of course. But a state of dreaming is, too.

I am safe here. But now I know, safety is never a constant. My world can shake and churn instantly. The question to chew on is... am I prepared for the world to fold inside out?

IV.

Why am I so dismissive about it now?
Even in that moment, a part of me wanted fright.
It's the normal reaction, am I wrong?

I tell myself: I saw no blood shed. I heard no bullets. The classroom was dark.
The darkness gnawed at all of us. Either I let it etch at me or let it caress me.
Moments I chose the former. I mostly chose the latter.

Was I allowed to feel nothing?
I felt like I hadn't earned the slight trauma that caged in me. I tried to move on with my life, and I mostly did.

But they kept asking me, "Are you fine? Are you fine?
I met the ones in the hospital, telling me they wanted life."

I'm one lucky son of a bitch. Perhaps the bastard should've taken me instead, for I still brush off my blankets as I arise, and croak about how I must walk to school in the tropical cold (with the added twist: they now demand my identification to let me in. I roll my eyes some more).

"Everyone handles pain a bit differently."
My pain is little to none. I almost forgot the whole thing ever occurred.
It's all normal. A few hindrances here and there, but it's all the same. Normal...

What did I survive?
Not losing my last hair of sanity? Because I'm certain I misplaced it in that dark room.

V.

If you really were a terrorist,
(what proceeds could villainize my name)
I sympathize for you.

Yes, you incited harm on brothers, fathers, and family.
Yes, you placed fear in the psyche of everyone around.
But you did not do it out of the blue.

I must scream a thousand times:
I do not vouch for what was done.
But at your home there is a war;
a constant back and forth for right and wrong.
You saw that we mixed ourselves in it.

You just wanted your own bed to sleep in.

In your eyes we threatened God.
You saw us using Him in vain
and thought us averse of something righteous and holy.
Against what is above all that is earthly.
Since this view was stabbed daily into your sight, then I confess, I feel your pain.

I know your pain without sharing your pain.

Your pain is all that you see, just like my pain is all that I see.

What is true pain, you ask?

Violence divides, no matter the case.
A life is lost, a scar is dawned.
You erased two loved ones off this earth,
and in turn, you forced the sheriff to cut you off, too.

Look at what you did. Look.
Your bullets did not stop a war:
they created one more.

Blue Angels

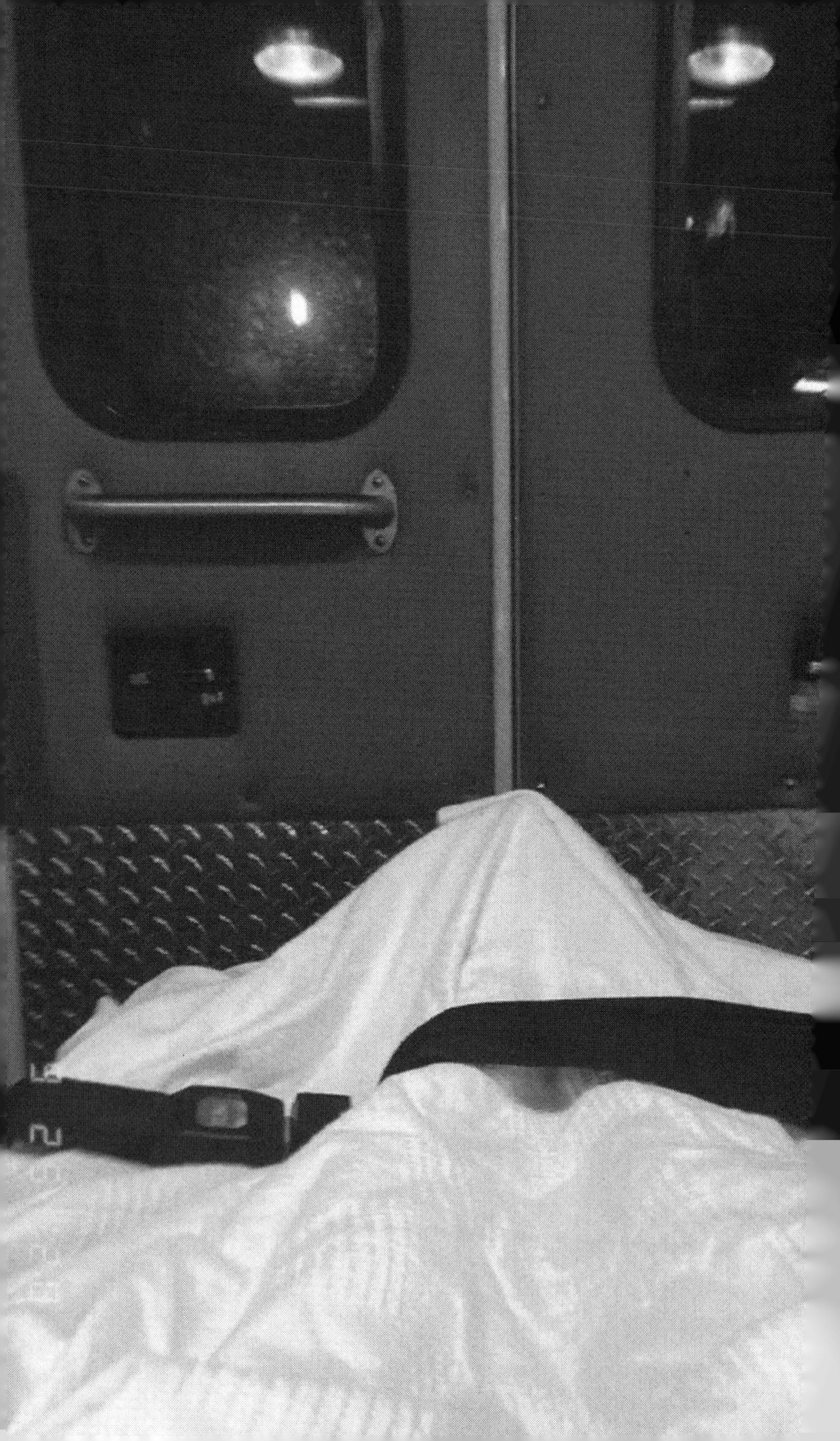

THE AMERICAN DREAM ISN'T WHAT IT SEEMS | 2020

AGES 18 & 19

I MOVE HALF-WAY ACROSS THE WORLD TO INTRODUCE MYSELF TO THE OTHER HALF OF MY IDENTITY, THAT OF MY AMERICAN SIDE. PERHAPS SHE WILL TAKE ME IN.

OUTSIDER. LOVELESS. NO GUARANTEE FOR A FRUITFUL FUTURE.
WHAT ARE YOU DOING HERE?

The Opportunity (To Inspire Oneself in Stagnant, Lonely Times)

FEBRUARY 6, 2020

I arrive in Virginia to start my job, away from the adrenaline and grind that filled my first few months of living in the United States. I am excited to embark on my new life, but I quickly realize that here, there is no adrenaline. There is no grind. I play Tori Amos's song 'Pretty Good Year' on repeat.

Nighttime is my time.
The moments before the waste; the waste washing the bore.

The bore, a bore indeed.
I flaunt it like a golden goblet—
as if I'm some artificial intelligence in the sunlight hours.

Mama Amos hums in a color,
navy blue,
though blue's the least I feel.
(Only since she sings to me:
"Well, let me tell you about America...")

I observe this nursery room, one I can barely squirm through.
Must be the day's collective load restraining me.

This dark ain't no navy, but it's quite the twin.
Hot stars glimmer not: my thoughts sub the twinkle.
Light ought to be light. It's bright, requiring broad shoulders.
My thoughts have come to light:

What's a home without some lovin'?
I caged my love in. None escapes, none enters.
'Tis in solitary confinement.
Though no punishment has been issued thus far.
Vacation time, so rest up!

The air settles its fatty excess all over me.
I was not informed it was capable of such.
Why not tell me? Why cache the details?
Let me in on your secrets. To hell with your surprises.

My skin eats it all up. I was not prepared.
I inch toward the start of the road.
An inch per hour is the speed limit you have all set.
I lug all this weight upon me. My muscles don't tense, but
release for extended periods!
I need the fat to melt to grease; excite my engine once again!

Distract me... turn me away for a while...
Turn me toward the other settings,
the ones which are not plain to the eye.
I choose a ladle and a pot.
I'll scrape off what you gave me,
and boil it myself.
It'll have nothing to do with any of you.
Selfish may I be, but 'tis a necessity.

In this virgin land,
the motions here are as a lake.
I expected a river.
I want to spew, spurt, and ravage
like a river does, then expand beyond!

(Only since she sings to me:
"Still, a pretty good year...")

The Summit

FEBRUARY 23, 2020

I've discovered the uncharted waters.
(Or more like, they discovered me.)
I predicted they were around this little nook;
how wrong I yearned to be, yet instinct corrected me!

The water is brown and littered, but no boat has glided through,
but some time — in no time — the prophecy had to bear fruit!

Let's start from scratch: the beginning.

Atop I was near heaven's gate. Not really, though— death had no role to play.
I basked in the yellows and gentle blue.
Nothing to hide from, nothing to run to.
Zephyrs cradled me as I neared the summit.

The exact coordinate of said summit? I was not aware.

The weeds nestled between the grass arms would always sort of whisper: no one's supposed to know.

"Copy that", but I was the least worried.
Steadfast I rode!
The altered state was impressive; it lasted for months and oh did my muscles relax. My eyelids closed,
and my world remained colorful; bright red and still some yellow.

Then my feet felt the earth turn jagged.

Then the wind tickled my feet.
I'm quite ticklish, you know—;
I convulsed and I—

am now on a boat, surrounded by dead water.
Isolating.
I bang into a rock, unforeseen: a pint splashes into my boat, and I gasp.
I've seen this before.

Hey, hey! Stop! No, no, no! Please! I beg you!

Another sharp thing cuts a wound in my boat, but I somehow land ashore.
It's all mud: slop all over my feet.
The grand escape, thought I, yet with each move
I sank deeper in brown till it mangled my crown.
All that my tongue licks, my ears ring, my nose detects, and my fingers claw at
is this: the uncharted waters
which were always on record.

Thought they were gone; like a second big flood
(or drought?)
but ignoring their spot does not force them up to a faraway place.
Even if that were so, rain would only fall again in a much broader target.

I must deal with the consequences;
this crept up on me with no warning.
Either I adjust: identify with the nature, or
try one more time to find a different arm to grab.

I wish I had never reached the summit.
It felt not like a summit
but more so a vast stretch of land that abruptly cuts off.
Couldn't I just have remained someplace there?

On Being Eighteen

March 16, 2020

A twist in my bones—
That of my two ankles— pines
For a timely day.
When marrow spurted and gushed
And my ribs swelled out, now lost.

To be of the youth,
To be of a higher stair;
A wishy-washy
Mind I now seize— for I'm the
Youth and higher stair, all one.

A barbed fence stands meek.
I've a dirt lair underneath;
My humble abode
Is in this grit you've patented
For me. To wander south? North?

I've no permission
To roam where I please. Do I
Astound you, really, (with the foreseen)?
To do as they do, comply,
Then brood on this: who are "*they*"?

Vibrancy, I lack:
My past has made sure of this.
Though now I see all
The waterways, their grandeur.
Still, I cannot blend the lines.

Must I lower hands?
Dig out the dirt from my nails,

Smack my lips, floss teeth
With this icy, charred blanket
And remain revered to you?
Should I leap over
This fence? Or weaken my knees?
My legs are stout; it's
A close call each grave attempt.
Back and forth; each and all hours.

That one acute barb
Always glares me up and down.
One day it'll act;
Bloody up what is still clean,
My flesh; soil it charred, icy.

Is that the sole way
To rid of these barbed bounds?
Sound a commotion
All along them, then mourn days
Of both scopes, desiring one (union)?

Your laws state: she's space.
Announce!: "She should not exist."
How is it truthful
That one's physical body
Should present itself in two

Polar areas
On the same ticking second?
Or to limit me
To either a newborn babe
Or woman internally?

A Prayer Awaiting

April 6, 2020

Months have come to pass without a proper word to You.
A year has gone since I sat down, with a table between us,
and interrogated You and Your supposed lovingness.
Only the two of us.

"The Most High who still kneels."
How true is that?
When all the world grinded smaller than sand, I
concluded: He rose off to better things. He's chastising me.
He thinks me unbearable. I deserve the cruel scorns from
the flesh. Maybe adulthood was this: to collect all waters
in a cycle inside you, then dump on the third count.

Maybe this new permanence is meant to strike you till death.
To never feel complete, or sane.
He preaches love. A hot, suffocating, but homey emotion.
He is withholding the unbound of love from me.

I deserve it.
I'm a demonic entity, born privy of my ability
to eradicate all original greenery to smithereens.
Therefore — oh honestly — I never seem to keep steady.
She and he are uninterested.
No signs of sympathy or care.
Not from the present or the future.
Not from the flesh or the heavenly.

These thoughts contained in me; —never were they to
skin against what You've chosen as the medium of life:
fresh, clean, choking air.

To even ponder — itch at — Your integrity
frightened me. I had given You a chance to share what
You truly rep, Your promises,
and yet,
in my tasteless, dull pearls You had not passed my test.

Here I was, boasting of Your glory and mercy, urging
others to turn to You;
but if anyone scraped long and hard enough, behind my
praise was a cry. I had no clue of glory, mercy. To be
frank, I felt not those, but quite the polarity.

My person differs now, but why is it still the most
exhausting task
to extend my jaw, close my eyes,
and form a single word intended for You to hear?
If the me from a year prior were correct in her
hypothesis,
you would strike me again.
Break me down till I'm brittle and unable to stand on my
two feet
like you had done so many times, for not having spoken
to You.

Yet all I feel is plain and content.

A lost lamb, I am. And I proclaim it!
To whom exactly? In the literal, no one nears;
but You, my God, see and hear what I do.
Every thought I think, every movement I chance.
Omniscient, You are so. I acknowledge that evermore.
Father, You only wish for my honesty.
You long for me to run back to where you reside,
but keeping faith is a difficult concept to practice.
I know You as this ruler who is to exist.

Yet, sometimes... even in the present I don't know if You are the Parent You brand yourself as.

You're aware of this, but maybe You'll be proud if I admit this to the material:
I wanted, again, to die last month.
And I repeated to myself: no one would notice.

I don't desire my death now. Though knowing me, the wanting will come again. And again. Again.

I despise how emotional and broken I am.

Then I'm reminded:
You've designed my code for a reason: for every word spoken by You has a set course to sail and it's never to waste.

I, myself, from my nerves to my brown shielding are a set code established by You. No mistakes were made.

My frail nature, however much I may want none of it, is all Your joy. You love it so much because You commanded: make her so. My pluses, my minuses, are all gaining towards this interconnection. It's a headache to imagine with my puny brain, but You bear it for me.

You love me, why? You love me. No ifs, ands, nor buts to add. Your simplicity perplexes me much!

Like a parent should, You have me crawl through the thickest mud to educate me. Enrich what knowledge I have thus far.

Like what a teacher once told:

God isn't what we — in our naïve, boundary-stricken containments — would consider pleasant all the time, but always is He ***perfect.***

Like what a preacher had stated:
Our faith in Him ought to waver, as feelings mimic the weather, but He is persistent and patient—
Our thoughts about Him will change, but His thoughts about ***us*** *never will.*
You are my Protector if anything. The definition will mold and vary day by day but:

If anything, You are my Protector.

Nineteen Candles

MAY 7, 2020

I should celebrate myself.
Preparation for that collected itself into years.
Naturally, it should.

I should have flicked the lighter
and caramelized the wick myself, for myself,
when my mom and pop's thumbs refused to.

Once I mustered up the bravado,
there I stood, aimless yet with a target in mind:
had the flame scrape its rabid lung onto my dry eyes.
For all that muttered 'no' to my invite,
I sent you a card with the tears my body could lay on the
sheet: a liquid thing, not invisible— but red ink.
No explanation needed. Vice versa you do unto me.

The candle wax creeps into my cake's pores.
Then seeps out, spelling: orphan, bastard, you rotten whore.

How should a cake I baked myself, for myself,
speak to me in such a way?
Crude and mannerless?
All that I have left is myself and this cake;
we both must party the night away!

O myself, this cake; it's no good for me!
All I would die for, murder a town for
are the people who tricked insanity to steer me.
The people who declared, "This girl is not mine!"
Next minute, "Why, she's all the world! Why does she ignore?"
The ones who transfixed me, then force fed a belief:
that I, a simple girl, was a blood borne madman.

I have this itching: that we all could plant our feet in one place, and I could exist near them— so near that I hear every tempo tick their clockwork system.
I would mash heaven and hell together to hear the words: but I loved you all this time!
These words in a range of alto, a belting wallow, a crack or two in the voices, a hiccup, ending in a mutual quiet.

The runaway, the good for nothing
who celebrated her birth anniversary
all alone for too long!
Physically, you all were present,
but only I rejoiced in my accomplishment
of reaching a checkpoint, a landmark,
of another year and counting.

'Twas only I who burrowed my toes in the carpet,
smiled slightly, blew gently
at what we determined to be symbols of an added year of life.

The orange, in its short youth, broiled with all its will, so much so that a quick poke could have sizzled a surface exposed;
the gust slapped the orange to an overcast cloud, gray,

and just like that, all your anticipation dropped.
The smoke. I could have been that. I tip-toed to that most days.

I had gambled daily with the proposition: must I like the candle, or the smoke?

The time nears when I must celebrate myself, truly and
utterly in lone company.
My first year far from home. (At least what the rest of
you determine where "home" was.)

I celebrate myself, with my very own cake, all for myself.
I do so because that is my right.
I celebrate myself and begin to love with a love more
pure-bred than an infant basking in her mother's arms
as I live for a right life and for my right to live.

The Lesson to the Girls

JUNE 3, 2020

She witnessed the rain scooting away from the sun.
Once the midday awoke her,
she thought, finally, "Why, I should write about this!"
'Impermanence' enjoyed her company, then.

To all the girls in line that stand between her
and myself:
gather round, gather closely...
I've a lesson to teach:

You think of yourselves as transparent, meek; a passer-
by; a revolution forming in the sewage, beneath the
rocketing streets.

You are not those in the negative connotation.
No one is.
You are dominoes tumbling, don't you see?
The 'Good mornings' you greet,
the scrapes your knees feat;
these all equate, and navigate
toward the field none of us will see.

We mortals with our organs sewn on
won't see the population holding hands!
Your efforts are not wiped off by tissue!
No, they are seen and added!

You are a burning car—
we all are on this outstretched highway.
The helicopters film you, but you will not locate the
footage.

The blankness in your eyes, the less than ten words you utter in a classroom—
yes, the fingers count those, too.
One teardrop in the sink, or a whole oil cart dumped in a bay
are all still mixed and sloshed in the sea.
All are a 'together'. Not to be excluded or singled out.

It shall be noted
by One,
then eventually by others who can clench your shoulders
and say, "Wow, do it again!"
Those words shall be said with conviction, not force-fed!

I am not hooting fanciful tunes. In plain, simply the truth.
The time to believe is not your now (my then), but
time comes when time ought to.
You'll know it, then, as true. As I do.

Not just to believe in Oneness,
but to skim out the edge and exclaim,
"I am not a see-through lace veil!
I coexist with all, and I deserve to!"

Nankurunaisa (Hardship Won't Come)

JUNE 15, 2020

Where is home for me? It's not in America. Okinawa has rejected me, too. The two parts of my identity, the two sides of my only coin, are against me.

Home — where often we would boast, "Hardship won't come!"
— introduced itself to me as Eden;
wherein I chewed up one too many apple pits
which my own acidity could not withstand.
I hoisted them in— no, I said out!
Those seeds colonized and mounded into a paste I am unable to scrape.
They bind to me like regrettable soul-ties.

"I am not a host!" Yet the output was a mere whistle-tune, but still, it fulfilled as a carrier!
Crumbs rode amongst it, thus I thought that progress had now logged.
Jokes on me:
The specks abraded my pupils —
I wane, for all the esteemed and wise
rely on vision, past and present.

A troublesome one,
always was, past and present:
I rub it deeper, and the metronome ticks its teeth.
A revelation never arises to poke the teeth instead.

"Hardship won't come."
I repeat, repeat, repeat.
"難来るないさ!"
I acclaim, adopt; acclaim, adopt.

I contemplated ink on me...
'Scrawl it saliently so the whole lot of us can see!'
The foreign people cannot dissect it;
how opportune, I shall form a new fiction!

"なん来るないさ!"
It is the gospel!
You all belt, and — unnoticed — I whisper.
I stretch my jaw to match your measurements.
The walls reverberate the tones of the masses.
So, in the mix, the masses I become.
The energy is quite the ecstasy,
but contagious it is not.
The glitz of my masquerade dims,
and the strings untie: soon to unleash the fallacy.
My jaw stiffens, and I cramp.

I exhort myself to pacify somehow.
Think back... what have I been taught?
Inhale.. ex...
Hell.
Hell.
I had consumed a product of Hell.

I have puked some out.
Discreetly! Discreetly! Discreetly?

The reverberations still flutter all around,
and the masses remain attuned.
The utter thought of discovery
renders me ill.

"なんくるないさー..."
To be of identity— how comforting, the thought!
Yet to completely envelop myself in this gospel...
"Nān kuru naī sā..."
I have eloped to another phrase:

"Hardship inherits us and will always follow us.
Hardship warps us."

This I outwardly chide!
Yet internally, beneath my carbon confines
the letters compose, erase, compose, erase.
The metronome goes at its strumming pace,
and I plead the words are never
noted by the masses.
My Home must be some place on Earth!

The Five

JUNE 17, 2020

Trigger warning: lynching

I heard it was five.
Another source says three—
the point being: one is one too numerous; one is
perturbing.

Suspended feet, dangling locks,
undulate in the hay fever like a wind chime.
A suspended blood rush amasses where gravity is found.
Folded-over gummy neck; that is not what is transcribed
in biology books.
Certainly not benign— not a genetic condition.

How should a human resemble a lily of the valley?
Creased from improper posture?
How unjust for him to be a life-like, tenfold sized rag doll.
His sand-grain cells amass where gravity is found.
His upper half void of juice, like a beaten lemon.
Crowd the dusty — now rusting — life forms into his big
toes.
His flux lines set to zero. Mangled, strangled.

Dangling while quietly ending.
Boiling lava, his saliva, went drip drip drip.
The last flavor he savored was not of the likes of blood,
not of sand,
but something of antimatter, of vacuumed outer space.

Robert Fuller, full of air which his body is unable to utilize.
Malcolm, Dom.
No, I'm afraid we are not done.

The report states simply, "Suicide."
I'm sure the three would counter the phrase.
Their humiliation is public to the naked eye:
They swing back and forth on oak trees, unwillingly.
To be nonliving, rocking adjacent to a living body...

Justification by the austere killers, the hiders:
"They were colored like a birthday piñata.
We do as we should, strike it till it shears.
Small paper cut,— we go by baby steps, of course— then
slam a bruise. Strike, strike, batter till it purples!
Contusion, now he's brown and violet;— oh, you thought
we were done?— slice, listen for some gurgles, a shriek,
thump, crash, thump!
Now red wine sprinkles on us!
This is a festivity,— and now we feast on the fructose!
The cherry on top: displaying our blood, sweat, and tears!
Or, aha!, should I say his?"

I recall a few years prior,
I sat in my drafty class as the only 'dirty one'.
The retelling of a century old article on lynching was
nearly sung to me.
I wanted to burst immediately.
All the others, stone-faced, did not smirk or frown.
What thoughts popped in their minds?
All my brain could muster was:
'At least they don't hang us, now.'
I wasn't aware. I wasn't aware.

I recall a few hours prior,
my coworkers and I convened in a tight room.
"How have you been?"
"Oh, these riots are dumb, plain as day."
"What about you, Sammi?"

"I have not been okay. None of this is okay. I—"
did not get any substantive words in.

"Let's keep this civil. It's difficult for everyone. Let's cut this short."
Cutting it short... we will see hanging men all over again.
The cycle is not cut short.
Their nooses were not cut short.
Your inane banter from the other day was not, oddly.

Let's keep this civil... I'm quite certain those three wanted civility. So, they complied.
Civility was not repaid.

How is it civil to allow humans to mirror a lily of the valley, a ragdoll, a beaten lemon?
A piñata colored brown, purple, and red!

Civil; your definition coats my esophagus with phlegm, ick!
We all desire a reliable civility. A vow; from the Reconstruction, prior and to now!
We shall never be granted it if we do not speak!
For those three, and all the others, pleaded!
So, we choose to mute them?

Like you mute me?

My First Heartbreak

JUNE 18, 2020

My fingernails rake through the base of my scalp.
Then the rim of my ear.
A squeaky shrill of exactness in each new syllable;
a worrisome up-tone at the end of each sentence;
each hiragana any native speaks evokes remembrance.

Of what? I can't point at one singular dot.
It's a conglomeration; the matrix, a jelly.
A lick of saccharine, that's what fashions the bite.
The aftermath is the expired, the one up for purchase on the shelf.

That's all that's in stock.
This is what I feed each new guest.
"How chagrining." Well, naturally!

Even more awkward, discomfiting:
Most would say their first rip from the guileless novel
is when a lover concedes infidelity:
whether literally or emotionally.
When they tell you you're no longer a revelry:
"You're just a plastic toy I've outgrown."

My blood blushed me as red as I could fathom.
The first gap that tailed me is a rare illness.
My peers inquired where the fill was.
I replied with a half-truth:
"She's attached to her birthplace and hates to travel."

I did not admit to the other fifty percent.
That sentence satisfied the question, so why would I detail more?

I'm the one you coddled in your arms.
I was an adoring, precious possession at the earliest.
I exasperated you, made you wipe off your sweaty head.
A day's work leaked into the night.
I would weep like I was dying, dying, dying.
Perhaps your revenge was meant to unfold.
Perhaps you were meant to build up my confidence that
you were the best employee, working your job well.
Then toss me to the sea, — a haste turn of events —
have me sink to the bottom level.
Perhaps you wanted me dying, dying, dying.

Distance, you prescribed to yourself— but you convinced
yourself a doctor told you so.
Then why do you suppress the reason? The ingredients?
Why not liberate it so the uncertainty precipitates,
and the settlement hangs in faultless alignment, like a
Newton's cradle?

I was reeled out. I swear I did not give consent.
I'm sorry your disappointment found itself back to you.
Your only defense was to be the offense.
Plow for ammunition, then sputter the rounds.

I am the reminder of your youth when you grew old.
I am quite the superfluity, I know, I know.
I bid my farewells as soon as possible.
You drank your third wine and drove past me, a hit-and-run.

"None of what you said was true. I'm sorry."
That's what you revealed a few weeks back.

I sincerely wish I could hit undo,
tap backspace several thousand times,
but those keys are invented. This is physical.

The remembrance is mostly acetous;
I can't scrub it off my taste buds.
A crueler portion of me salvaged the vinaigrette dressing.

You say your love is eternal,
like God's greatest gift.
So why didn't you love me
when I neighbored you constantly
and from afar?

American

JUNE 23, 2020

Land of the free, home of the brave.
These grassy grounds are that which house the free, the brave.
These words sound to me like a stanza I recite for a grade.

I am at its birthplace, not far off from humble Jamestown.
Outside should smell like the plains, should smell like air freshly found.

Maybe I shall own the star-spangled banner.
For a second, I think I designed it:

American by blood, by name.
Yet once the plains sucked in my shoes, I felt its mud, not the plains.
Others view me an immigrant when I, by nature, have 'American' in my role...
Why, that's a true American! An immigrant always, forevermore!

I wince at the sight of division, but I really wince at identity:
The highest threshold of such a citizen is to feel division within.
Reluctance to cognize the turned head, when identity was lost from thievery and genocide;
when the priority was economic upbringing, not welfare of the ones who tried.

Shall consistency throughout the centuries equate to a band aid?
Fireworks free themselves during the anniversary of freedom,
but the day has not yet arrived.
They may drop me off from a bus to assassinate the rowdy, the ones up too late.
To silence their sparks which they plead to know not where they originate.

"There's nothing we can do to extinguish chaos."
That's the folklore in these parts.
The sentence was rearranged differently in my youth, but I now know its root.

The star-spangled banner waves at the center of the universe, and we must all praise a Hallelujah to it.
No one is exempt, we must go through with it!

My sentiment is defiant; my lowest sentence I receive may be that I am still in my teens.
If I be banished, I'll be a true American,
so that I am brave in a home where I am free.

Memorial of the Living

JUNE 23, 2020

For my Grandma and her late brother, for all the Okinawans who passed away during the Battle of Okinawa, and for the posterity that lives on, keeping the island alive.

Baāchan, you're alive!
Three-quarters of a century, yet you still have all
four limbs.

We appear unlike— I bet you're in disbelief when the
doctors repeat, I'm in your bloodline.
Baāchan, you're alive: but you're in mental decline.

Remember when you were a spectator at my sport
games?
When most of the family only hid the house key and I
knew nothing of the basement door?

I weep at the notion of stumbling back to square one.
To think that all I lived for has no permanent grounds.
That's where you are, yet maybe for you it's the perfect
route.

Are you unable to recount the red flags waving?
The days that compressed non-plural, and the red sun
setting?
How many beetles did you have to scour and plug your
nose for before bracing to eat?
Do you remember your brother? If so, I hope only when
he stuffed himself plenty.
Red sun, which couldn't do its primary gig:
burgeon some purple potatoes to feed the macilent kids.
子供だったのに... my Baāchan!

Did you think you were going blind
when the white flags flapped like doves in the summer fight?
Where did you find the strength to rebuild the island from pure starch,
when my chopstick arms can barely hold myself up when I conclude life's a farce?

Baāchan, I'm learning the battle didn't end on the twenty-third, seventy-five years ago—
it's a continuation, it's what every day is.

You toil the toughest fight—Baāchan, you're alive!

*子供だったのに (Kodomo datta noni) – you were only a child

The See-saw by the Seashore

June 25, 2020

The see-saw, that wooden board that teeter-totters.
The creaking of its fixture besieges me like famished ants.
One little ant amounts to six of these:
tap tap tap and again.
Try a whole colony to the power of eleven;
once they're done, they transform you: pruny, sour,
dry— like a pack of raisins.

I had to get away! Far away!

I was five when the see-saw was a carnival ride.
For hours, we would rocket to the sky then plummet near the ground.
I was five when that was a good thing.
I would only return if it remained so,
but you can't revert to childhood's hour.

The see-saw by the seashore— they thought it wise to abhor.
What did I do to deserve derision, division?
Within me I teetered from contempt to ripping off my skin.
All because of you. All from you.

I was born lightweight, so my own form could not eject nor plunge.
When I was down, you were up—
scrutinizing my every twitch, my occasional itch.
My lone authority was my vision,
but most times, curiosity got the best of me.
I could not protect my one power.

Our eyes would meet and ah! my stomach would fall sick.
I could not just up and leave, for you would smash to the ground if I did.
Tomato sauce, all on the floor. Oh, my stomach
would fall sick.
I would smash to the ground if I did.

When I was up, you were down.
When I was up, I could not fall.
You would scrutinize me still, as I dangled my stubby legs and wailed for a rescue.

I turned my head and saw another victim: flying up then drowning through air.
'Yes, she will understand! Finally, I'm not alone!'—
and she told me I was nutso, flowing off the grid:
"Just take it in! This is what love is."

Some days, the see-saw would be like it was back then,
how it originally was, how it was constructed to be:
plain fun.
You thought 'plain' wasn't good enough.
Tragedy is the best excitement we will dream.

Your leg strength fizzled, ushered little.
The log leveled out, and you slumbered.
'I have to get away! I have to get away!'

Far from the see-saw by the seashore.
I do miss its landscape. No, no— here I am sheltered and safe!
Crackle, crackle, screech.
The famished ants still tap-tap their hair strand legs and say that I am weak, and that the see-saw still creaks.
Always I hear it before I sleep.

Reach

JUNE 26, 2020

Reach not: squeeze, clamor, rage!
Then the product will rest on your lap, as fate has said.

The Mongol Nomad
(Who Ruins Everyone She Meets)

JULY 1, 2020

I'm in a game of hopscotch:
island hop from lard to parched.
Mark my words— O, the blonde strands of the steppe
shall strip the black of my virgin hair.
Deteriorate; write it in as permanent residency.
I trot a rabbit's dance, pretending the floor's lava.
Water, water? Why, none dares a mental breakdown
'round these parts.

Insufficient dust cannot cultivate greens,
so, I ravage the life that I herded: breast milk and horse meat.
Kill off my only friends. Slaughter them daily for breakfast and supper.
I'm an absolute sucker for obliteration: set off the egress and explode my progress,
glide toward another atmosphere, only to be slapped to the humblest floor— like an Icarus reborn.

I'm in a game where it's only back to level zero.
If I stumble across some villagers, I loot and slaughter them, too. Woo them, entertain them, till I'm bored.
I shall ooze across the continent, trail my victims and own all.
All's mine for the taking because I said so.
Despicably, unknowingly. You agree, unwillingly.

A squeak inside me will sway my moral compass correct,
and I will dwindle like crumpled paper, once more.
Never to be heard from again, never to be thought of
unless to be a paragraph in a molding textbook.

The Siren's Song
(Sung Where His Grave Was)

JULY 6, 2020

I am a little old sailor:
rowing, floating around the clock.
The 'be-all and end-all'—a misnomer, quite.
Who knew of a more perfect sphere?
One of intact exactness?
Gently down the stream, then soon ushered!
My destination umpteen, yet my feet may fail no matter.

Hours I had devoted to prayer: for the savage blue to solidify.
Or at least a stick from a stable ground to reel me ashore.
My, I tire. I pray then for a three-sixty-degree screen.
The salt tightens the nut and bolt, and I am tucked in— a liquid babe.
What am I to make of this comical wonderland?
I am a fluid: boil me, peg me. I care none for the plight!

An opera ballad screeches from a savior, throttling my inner ear,
but ah!— it is a sort of sign!
I paddle and squall some tears.
Merrily, merrily... life is but a dream!
I shall embody it, and profit; I am free!
Merry-go-round, three-sixty degrees...
Meanwhile, I croon the song she had reeled me with.
Nearer to my wonder! My lover! My—
siren!
Siren?

Gulp.
'Tis the dreaded me, engulfed.

But little did she know, I was always a brain-dead thing.
I had tapped my nails on my boat in a brisk repetition,
for a hue of green to say yes,
but have you known a four-leaf clover to sprout in the
ocean? —But I digress.
To the posterity which hears this gasp, the final ring:
Wake to every morn! Life is but a dream!

Half-Oki

JULY 10, 2020

"Ooh, exotic cougar! Spicy, I can't help but fan myself!"
Well, the only 'exotic' trait about me
is my inability to translate with clarity the thrills my mom exclaims.
Or the drawn-out half-hours I exhausted to iron my ringlets to pin straight hair,
so that I could declare, with hardihood: "The 'blackness' ain't there!"

"起きて." I wish my tongue **would** wake up—recount what was lost after I started the first grade.
"沖." I am an islander— I think. Islanders can float, or swim. If the water flushes above **my** stomach, I know I would vomit:
the mere imagining of the bottom-most level of the ocean;
the anglers! Fangtooth, and the vampire squid!

Those horrors would shear me bite-sized. Me, the imposter: undeserving of a bite of the rich history.
I'm letting it go to waste: the corals are listless, with paling skin.
The bystander I am, kicking back and watching them pleading for mercy, for an extension.

I kick back and hear the inane:
"Look at her bizarre mane! She must be Hawaiian or Brazilian!"
I slacken my fists to openness, answer, and I am met with a, "No way! That can't be correct!"
Have you met my parents? How would **you** know then?

"You're a pearl! An oddity!"
I'm called a wretched mutt by the real pearls here:
the real terrorist threat, who fashion themselves like it's Halloween all year.
They're an oddity, indeed. I shrink myself around them, and comply with a simple, "OK, OK, OK."
Around them, my life hangs by a thread. To them, I am the threat.
I admit, I suffer from fatigue.
I slumber for hours on end, never-ending. I wake up and it's like I never went to bed.
I'm either half-awake or half-asleep. Never a fully risen or wholly dead being.

I'm of a spectrum, and the tick goes left-right on its own, but I'm always 'too right' for you, even when I educate how it's not my fault.
I'm a teabag left in the cup for too long, and you snap at me like I'm the waiter: "I asked for lightly brewed, not this over-saturation, this dark murk!"

I'm a pearl, an oddity.
If I were blacker, the inundation of n-words would daily occur. Niceties, nourished skin? No, not those.
Nasty pig nose, nappy cotton-field fro? Yeah, more like so.
If I were more yellow, I would hark the unoriginal remarks:
"Chinky slit eyes, railroad worker. Should've been stuck in a camp."

"First world problems, whatever!"
Why yes, this was the first of my problems:
My ojii-chan almost disowned me because I am 'dirty'.
My dad barely understood me when I was a tearful baby.
My mommy bites her tongue because her English steers sideways.

My own mind muddled itself, and for years I couldn't communicate: "I'm not okay."
To all who regard me, either in praise or in disbelief, recite this, and let it seep:
"I'm either half-awake, or half-asleep. Never a fully risen or wholly dead being— no, I can't change a thing, but these dual features are what fuse me. So, I agree to this perplexion, indefinitely!"

*起きて (okitte) – wake up *沖 (oki) – first kanji in 'Okinawa'/ water

Maryll, Let's Bow in Prayer Together

JULY 13, 2020

For Mari. For everyone who needs this prayer.

I thank God for the chance of my soul.
I thank Him for the hikes I trudge on the hill.
O Lord, even when I purposefully hunger,
Even when I rid of hydration from my inner layers and out—
Lord, You revive me every time.

The daily task is toiling, I dare.
Yet, You walk with me,
Pray with me, till I'm out of air.
I say the damage is done, but my God,
You keep me here, and everywhere.

Heal the wretched that cast despair unto me.
Heal them so they, too, are in Your forgiving palms.

Clear her mind, Lord. Teach her, so that she may flourish
As You planned her to.
It is written, and so it shall be said.

You forgive me and all the wicked every time.
Speak in us that we have You—
That we inherently *can* love one another.

I plead, soften our inner turmoil.

Amen.

The Sky's Hypocrisy

JULY 14, 2020

I am at a point in my life where I am mentally content and capable of financial abundance, but a voice in my core tells me that I, for one, don't deserve that success, but more prominently, that money will not make me happy. A void consumes me and I'm afraid nothing will ever satisfy me.

I am but a grain, gluttonous for the milk and honey.
A sweet nothing on this vast, crass beach.
The sky's the limit; I cannot reach it, ever, as this.
Though, it is the same as I;
the woken hours are yellow-gold.
Say, why don't we conflate?

The sun shimmies and stutters;
she is an indecisive, spoiled child: reviving Herself in the east, crawling up the ladder, only to decay in the west.
Rinse and repeat.
What an awful role model, you are.
My brain curtsies in your wake, secreting serotonin at the sight of you: how acquiescent I am!

I lust for all, all, all; I reject the fall.
O Sun, you present shame to the empyrean scape.

You are the highest link, looming over us and all of me.
Powdering your dust, a spring cleaning; why all on us?

I, the contrasting umbra, yearn for the color I'll never be:
A true yellow, like you. (But are you really true? For you don't give a damn, and you're lazy, too.)
I've been trampled by mere flip-flops, splashed upstream then to low tide.
Now that I am liquid-free, you lead me astray!

Green can't buy happiness, but abundance means I'm liberated! My slave story concluded! The end!
Still poor, yet well off enough to purchase flexibility and release; misery is a solitary confinement cell: a white wall, restricting.

Haha! This is a cycle. Just stupid!
Your ultraviolence bestowed on me, again— huh, aren't I lucky?
All in your vision are reflected in pristine detail,
yet all I see are penumbras under your deceitful umbrella—
which is all I strive to own, but I cannot claim it, ever, as this.
You birthed me without my consent, and I fall victim to your dry, unrelenting joke.
Is this a gamble to you? Bet on my chances that you swipe my earnings?
What is a win to you? What is one to me?

You could give a damn what I wonder.
You are not blue, like serenity. You shift from purple to tangerine.
Yellow's cousin blushes red, and I won't hesitate to say:
You are more of the fiery Red Sky than God's shelter-in-place.

So why don't we conflate? You and I are the same.
Even in my transformed, woken state — cleansed of all my past impieties —
my gut acid still bubbles and pops, cramping for more riches.
What is worth this circus if even once I obtain it, I still am a shadow under you?
I can't decipher your true pigment, nor mine.
I cannot touch the sky, ever, as this.

Persistent Voice

JULY 15, 2020

Trigger warning: strong language, self-harm, anxiety, intrusive thoughts

My life! It's finally riding the upslope! I seize the *fucking idiot! You haven't made any progress! Don't forget where you came from: grease and grime.*

day! I'm a free hostage from my traumas, and I'll take advantage of that! *full advantage... you always use people. Therefore, many abused you. That's why no one will ever really love you.*

I'll try out different business ventures! Why should I be strapped to the menial 9 to 5, when I could be a *capitalist money-hungry bitch. You're so vain. What the hell will money help you with? That won't make you happy. And you'll never be fulfilled.*

successful, independent woman? I want to prove to myself that I'm capable of *scarring every person you choose to open yourself to. You're either vanilla bland or a bitter melon gourd. Just do away with yourself, please. You'll do everyone a favor.*

impressing even myself! I barely skimmed free from the guillotine in my teen years, and I survived! *and surviving is all you will ever do. Always starving, quenching, poking your skin with knives but* ***being too pussy to stab yourself till the blade shears all the way through.*** *You'll never really live.*

I still have my friends; they're the closest resemblance to a "family"! *stupid bitch, you really think they're here to stay? they just feel bad for you: you're FORCING them to talk to you. It's rude if they don't. Why do you always hold people captive?*
Maybe I'll shock my family, too. They are proud of me sometimes, I'll admit... *but you are a bothersome crybaby to them.* ***You know why your mother left you to suffer by yourself for so long?*** *Because you stole her youth from her.* ***You almost caused your father a stroke*** *because your lazy ass never did as he asked.*

Yet... they have pushed and pulled repeatedly. I'm just a yo-yo to them. *yeah, that's right. and you'll never impress them. even when you're affectionate to your sister, she's nasty back. when you distance yourself because you try and guess what she wants (a people-pleaser, but you can't even do THAT well), she accuses you of being close to sociopathic. That's what you are. Void of any real empathy.*

Why have I been thrown out so many times? *people have been through much worse. at least your parents didn't touch you. screams. it's just noise. grow the fuck up. see? you're being selfish, feeling like you're the worst person in the world. you're not number one in anything.*

Everyone's going to leave you, just like your family and your trusted friends did. Just deal with it; you were born for this.

Persistent voice! Leave me the hell alone! I want to open myself up and *know that I will never detach from you. Just as you annoy the shit out of everybody, I do the same to you. I'm of the karma embedded in this Earth.*

be what God wants me to be! And you— you are not of Him. You are of Satan. ....

I know you want me in everlasting anguish, to beg to dispose of you, but I shall unleash my strength over you. *Strength. ha. and whatever will that be?*

I'll store you in my pockets and dissect you. That way, I can fully extinguish you.

My Child from God

JULY 19, 2020

For Mari.

How can that version of me,
exempt from the rouge of menstruation,—
Is rouge the word? Perhaps rust will do.—
cosset for the pure and callow? Never
once affixed; never were they my progeny.
Yet adored for; my thumbs would depress against
their cheeks, praying for a response:
a pulse beat, or a carillon-bell giggle.

How can my present self,
capable of spitting out a perfectly packaged life,
avert away from the sight of a spitting baby?
Once I spot *it*, no longing, no nurture
erupts! Just another wild animal, it is.

I am my mother's daughter;
she once was me in a child-like way:
unequivocal, and would embosom all my corners
till my wallow dispersed, and I arrived normal.
What a while it has been: what *air* has even poked my
sides? Little effort it takes!
Perhaps she passed on the generational curse.

It was as if a stork transported in my place:
I am almost a Virgin Mary, I swear— quite chaste.
You spilled your despondency, laid it whole on the table.
A revelation: you and I aren't so antithetical.
A burst! It piqued!
Some other mother trilled a song in my still heart:
"*Irayohei... irayohoi...—*"

The proceeding line I translated in my head:
"*My dearest child, don't you cry...*"
No more shuffle; I repeated to hear the start:
A blessing from Heaven, you are born into this world.
My baby, though you are not of my flesh,
you are mine to seize: wholly, entirely.
Why are we explained: the unconditional bounds lie in
those we are bonded to by organs?
Perchance, I have been, all this time, connected to you.
Both of what we relied on disregarded our necessities.

My desire to shield you from the whipping
winds of your own withstanding is intense! So immense!
If I can manufacture a sort of equilibrium
and nullify your expanse coffer,
then prying my own heart to release and constrict
shall be what I live for.

Chocolate for My Body

JULY 21, 2020

A poem for my anxious body. Even when my physical symptoms combine forces with my mind, I still love my body for allowing me to live another day.

Why do you hanker a detestation from me?
Even when your phantom foot pulps my neck,
that vital connector,
and my life-heavy gas squirms past your pressure to free
itself, like a floppy tuna fish,
I don't hate you.

I intake, intake with no breaks.
I soak all life in, then you bash me again:
I assume a heart attack, but I am nowhere close to
faltering age.
Your tart liquid unfurls, contaminating my oxidation,
my gains.

Even when you jog my enshrouded memory
of the near impalings when the glint of the steel
fluoresced all white and you thought I could not see,
I am reminded of my muted voice and my heart
uppercutting against my chest in protest.
I thought we had a mutual understanding and a
handshake?
A near panic attack you fostered.
Nearly saved, but the evocation bludgeons my brain,
maiming a chunky muscle mess.
Ugh, the light years to scrub it all!

Even when you parch the rear of my esophagus,
my swallows are of a low pH;
So sour, like a decayed, ant-feasted lime. I imbibe it,
confounding it for water.

Mama Amos chants a tune...
It's almost an alarm: What you say, I don't find agreeable,
yet I catch your shrieks in the quietest of nights.
You are an embryo, undeveloped and desiring some
mothering from me.
Well, I don't hate you.

I sample that chocolate, the only treat in my bag.
the one 'embossed by the Belgian coat of arms'.
You rotate the knob on the stove to simmer the pot of
vinegar boiling in my stomach.
For we vowed to love eternally,
from womb to death tombstone.
We deserve our favored tastebud to reawaken and
present itself as existing.

One and Yet Different

JULY 23, 2020

You, only a year older, have been with me since I first
saw the hospital white light.
He subjected us both to identical warps:

Useless. Lazy. Never will be anything.

We both listened obediently, embracing those illusory
truths in.
Not knowing what to do, that was all we did.

The mutual strangles, the manic head throbs...
I trusted your inner warfare mirrored mine.

A couple seconds... contemplating. I speak—
And you transitioned to the second floor without me.
Now I'm the selfish one, not abandoning the thought!

How am I to interpret that? Your reaction saddens me.

Alone, I walk through the molt, still.
Frail, yet a permanent glue of the strongest sorts...

We are one, yet our prominence drifts.
An impossibility of sorts...

My Cherries, My Peach

JULY 23, 2020

These cherry fruits dangle
off my lobes— I'm near past my restraint to implode.
I've listened to your deafening whispers in excess:
"Inexperienced, emaciated toothpick...
When will she allow a bite of those ripe, fat drops?"

I've seen many sticks rouse to the jump
then jab jab jab others with little remorse.
Why such inhumanity for momentary juice?
No longer syrupy mead... more like bile, or chain rust.
Thirst for water instead!

What if I revealed that perhaps mine
aren't fully grown?
Numbered years define almost nothing!
You fiddle my jewelry between your fingers, yank it like
you'll tear my ears off, causing more than one bloody
pool I'll have to get rid of.
Trick, as if I'll submit to your phalangeal pressure.

"What about the peaches sat idle in the corner?"
What about them? What business binds you to those
supple nuances? You're not allowed in that quarter!
I tend to my garden— 'tis a part of my life contract.
You itch all over, confused by my commitments.
Well, whatever. We agree to disagree.

A pruny craisin prude,
or a pummeled, irretrievable plum scattered across;
both vile shames! I may as well
choose my own title.

Only the deserving shall indulge in a bite— or a meal? Only once my entirety, not just a few fragments of the field, is prime for harvest.

Backwards

JULY 24, 2020

Direct, direct.
Perhaps what will plop below won't be so imaginary.
I regard it not; I want to unleash!

From the first I've written, I've known...
Nothing nothing nothing is permanent.
Why am I so fervent, so maddeningly indulgent
In all the scopes I choose?
People people people people
Subtract four... I'm left with zero.
Swish the mouthwash around, then out!
A castaway, automatic shots...

So many barriers in my way—
I shoved them on the field on my own.
I wonder why? why? why? why
Can't I hold myself accountable?
Where are my limitations?

If I find myself back in that horrid, haunted place,
Back to the root of all evil,
It shall be based on the laws of history.
Science, reliable, depends on the recorded.
I am abstract, inestimable, like the arts.

What use is art to this impossible calculation?

What Do My Memories Taste Like?

JULY 26, 2020

What do *my* memories taste like?
There lies on my tongue—
an atomic bomb:
a purported speck, with no chicken pox skin situated upon such.
I spat it out; I wobbled on and on, stomping the microscopic intensity into the sludge.
No one sees; how pleasant...

My shoe's underside slit it — a paper cut broiled to the infinitude degree —
preposterous conundrum! *Slam!*
I fulminate! I screech, the needy baby I am!
My guttural heave strews in the wind:
deformed limbs on the newer generations, an abysmal thread.

Supposedly bland, but then: a guzzling bleed from you and I gush on and on; but oh, was it needed!
Listen to my writhing! Soak in my curdling roaring!

I am the mafia mastermind, but I plead to guilt!
The vandalism cannot be grated, but I will
revamp, spot clean, and hunt for a vaccine.
I cannot cure a scored *scar*, but rest assured:
I will endeavor to solidify the *clot*.

Under the Smoke Pit

July 29, 2020

I shadow you to that wooden smoke pit in the parking lot.
You prate a mundane topic; you're a record player needle unreleased.
"Got nothing much going for me." There.
Summarization complete.

So vain, and the gastric galore you've whipped up for me is propane leaks and cigarette nicotine.
That prowess in your possession is the sole generosity you'll ever offer.

Externally, I'm bred to be the night.
I overwhelm you, although I'm a hushed disturbance.
Lungs squelch; no longer can belt.
Wrung out insides; in three scores I'll truly undergo charred body parts all throughout.
Others join this rowdy bore, and I must outlast!

"White privilege!—" Oh? Now you've arrested my wandering mind.
"—is a hoax! We're all poor, dirt grown. Why am *I* the victim? What if I said black people were—"
Sir, with all the politeness I somehow still obtain:
I've officially blocked you out.
I can't last. This is not a place for me to stay!

I'm crammed, jam-packed
beneath this wooden atrocity.
Helpless, doltish! I can't drive away! All I do is rely and tipple your gawks!
Diseased air! I'm squished!
Secondhand smoke is all I smell!

We slogged through the elimination and the schooling
to arrive here: the land of opportunity.
The motto on the outer shell claimed: we embrace
diversity.
Rotting and nestling in the center: the sickness reigns
rampantly there.
Do I remove myself; omit? Or do I endure to solve; fix?

I am not an *other*, sir; simply *another*.
I comprehend your sentiments. We're all dirt grown.
Yet your inability to reflect all the perspectives till we
reach at least (*the very least!)* the mantle
is of a hypocrite's heart.
I plead politely: hear my hushed existence, please...

Better Days Are Coming

JULY 30, 2020

For Rachel.

「A mess, a future
darkened with cerulean
crayon-wax, cohered
to you: an attestation
of a ceaseless soap op'ra. 」

Yet warm palettes array themselves in the box!

You, my darling, are
not meant to exist among the morning of the dead,
where marine dribbles its moping and drool;
not meant to live a dragonfly's span: six months, cruel.

The following day, you still chose the balmy maize
brightening half of the Earth's blue-green glaze.
I'll say, the sun appears more like you.
Babe, I'm certain of the promise for better days!

Dissociation

AUGUST 2, 2020

Sociopath almost, roaming out of the path.
What was I to be? A fuming tyrant,
or a weeping, weary twine string?
A girl with a bobbed cut— repugnant.
Ugly duckling
who could not follow Mama duck properly.

Her arms stretch a thousand miles:
Her lacquered talons ram into my vitalities.
I can't see your new come art piece: I only endure
the wrath!
The voodoo doll, I am: constant prodding till I froth white
out of my mouth and sag.
Why can I only see most of my quiddity surging away?
No longer animate, I am of a body of a stream.
Swish, swish. Drift...

I am not even such! I am expansive and endless:
the Pacific Ocean.
All my life, it was my next-door neighbor, but now I label
it a foe.
Let's sign the armistice, officially— conclude a new
normal:
Motionless emotions... an unusually shiny attribute.
It has velcro teeth! Stitch it onto me!
Finally, an abiding accessory!

No depth of a sea's bottom:
hampered with the population's tears impregnated
with salt.
Who wants high blood pressure at a juvenile age? Or a
burdened *thump thump* in the heart?

The equator's heat is familiar, too.
Yet no warmth sheds on me, and actually—
I resigned to forgetfulness of
how depriving dehydration really is.

This symmetry thrills me, quite.
I have always been on the brink of mania: shot to Heaven
or sleeping right above Hell.
I am at home, yet a sensibility, so paltry,
shouts for a plea for aid.

This is not normal... you've got to search deep inside—
My soul's made of coal. A bore, more and more.
Tasteless and so far gone. Like my mama is.
She'll never return, so how is it possible I will too?

Last resort: hunt for anything! Then kill, kill.
What? How could I do such a task?:
So that I evince I am competent and worthy
of humanly existence: finally see a bleed
flow out... and spark a teardrop.
Then my own.

Isaias

AUGUST 6, 2020

Melatonin deficiency: is that doctor-invented?
What is the lesser of the two evils, tell me?
Slogging through the hours, or my jump-scare scenes
romping while I hibernate?

Maybe I am Aurora's relative, the one of royalty:
oppugnant to the literal definition of her name.
All I see are black out curtains, expunging even twinkles.
Crepuscular bath bomb fog, pervading my tub water;
it spotted me with blackheads; perhaps I am now the
grossest type: sticky sebum.

(For how am I hygienic if the only 'tub' I rest on is a
mattress?
Life is not cushiony forever! Bruise my posterior some!)

All I cognize is the color girdling all, of tire skid marks.
The memory of tropical fruit themed apricity— unheard
of.
The morning promise, dwindling by the day.

Why did no one unveil the cipher?
Just a: no need to come into work, you can rest a little
more.
I rejoiced while they snickered.
Isaias, you presumed swooner. You suctioned all the air.

I learn of your lightning thuds— zapped!
me up! Sirens! Whooping coughs!
"Take cover in shelter!"
I furl into a yarn ball, spherical and soft,
And cramp myself in my stuffy closet.

I have no food in the fridge, and I live in my own company.
(Curse them! Why did no one unveil the cipher?
There he was: Isaias, a knotted cesspool of his victims' dying breaths.)
To be lively in wake, the ultimate vexation.

You can't play tricks on me, you little boy.
I disregard your haunts, breezy taunts.
If you play darts with window glass shards, and
mince me till I'm ground beef, then I still won't care.
I am already edging into a comatose condition.
Nudge in that last one percent.

No time for vacillation. Either escape route is a dead end no matter.
Hypersomniac from now on and its letters are a scarification mod.

Isaias, you presumed swooner, you indeed spell on us a faint.
Distorting trees, flailing around poor human bodies.

I purchase the lottery ticket— one more chance.
I jolted my body-pillowed self upright, and I saw:
Afternoon orange decanting onto my floor,
and the branches on the wooden giants billowing only slightly.
—but a prediction of your multiples emits on the channel.
(Yet, manmade technology is so limiting, and in many instances, we are far off! I'm betting, betting.)

Isaias, you presumed swooner: I tackle against your odds, every day. One day, you'll truly dissipate.

I Am But Your Loathsome Daughter

AUGUST 19, 2020

Botulinum toxin is our automatic decision:
the most potent on the planet;
detected in the molding cans and—
coincidentally! in her genetically impossible plump lips.
I am but your loathsome daughter.

The start of every new year, you'd buy a luxury car.
I'd cower in the backseat, you: drive upfront, eyes affixed to your phone.
(No, you read that right: not the 'road'). The tires (or was it I?) would screech till we parked.
        You —
        and I — could never steer
        a manual stick shift vehicle.

Botulinum toxin is our automatic decision.

You cheated me out of a thousand dollars.
The only possibility of repaying my
        (your?) dues is to flee to the red-light district,
        join a secret sex cult, then sway
        the members into hurling bills at me.

I am but your loathsome daughter.

My phone is on silent whenever you type in my number.
My thoughts, however, go at it with my punching
        bag of a brain: if I answer, he'll holler—
        converse about his plain day. Ugh! What to do?

Botulinum toxin is our automatic decision.

You and I wear only dusk— clear as day.
For eons I ached to sever my association to the garden of shadows which you sewed my seed into.
To pride myself, or to bleach out my eyes to the entrapment?
Either-or, you disapprove. No certainty from me or you.
I am but your loathsome daughter.

For some time, I wanted the true ending:
suicide.
To dispose of you— actually, even grander of a wish.
(Said from me? Or from you?)

I bow my head and shut
my eyes for my Forgiving Creator, but how can I
    align with His rectitude when I refuse to
    pardon (my?) your own laundry list of wrongs?

(Whose words were those?
Whose deep voice fogged the wintry room?)

Botulinum toxin is our automatic decision.
I am but your loathsome daughter.

That Once A Month Thing

AUGUST 22, 2020

Happy 57th year of life, Tori. Unfortunately, my cramps were horrible on this day, which prevented a full celebration from me. Yet, my agony and your lulling voice in 'Yes, Anastasia' inspired me to go with the flow with my writing instead of my usual uprightness that normally guides me. This is the result I conjured up: one of my classic streams of consciousness pieces which only took twenty minutes to write.

"So, what is your gender?
I landed in a web of infatuation as I listened to your voice notes:
husky, I can hear your six-pack in your throaty vibrations.
Yet you mention you wet the bed, so maybe you're a child?"

You are like me— mishearing song lyrics.
I'm bedridden. My knees are sunken with water.
If I walk, the ground will simulate an earthquake, and my bile will splash out of the bucket!
So, stop! I am no supposed breadwinner!

I am a laze with no urge to wallop.
There are the cheetah scythe nails spiraling its clutch in my guts again. Oh how they gyrate!: my stomach is a washing machine window, showcasing my grimy uniform.
No detergent in this world can exterminate the splotch!

Is this the nearest to an electric taser sensation?
Certainly, I'm not having a punishment bestowed on me?
Am I to be on the run, hunted in a highway police chase?
Who, what, when, where, why?

I'm in the far corner, shut out. The five-minute time-out.
The older folk disapprove of the modern softcore ways:
they slither out the belt from their breast high pants and
itch to whip me!

Whack! on my abdomen. Must I breathe in or out?
Twelve times a year, this fated penalizing.

I've already soiled these ornate hotel sheets—
last time it was my new business attire. That's too bad—
(interpose the customary sigh)—
white's my only flattering color.
Money is flung
out the window once again.

The boys cannot simmer down when I sit up
and a red sun shadows on the chair.
"That's from her 'down-there'!"
The provenance could have been
the roughhousing scuffs on your bare
knuckles! Cousins, they are!

Either some entity tears me or I crush
under some rotund pus-filled foot, stomping all of me.
Any pleasurable wading is asking for the highest form
of scorn.
So then repeat the birds and the bees tale,
then uncensor it; for that R-rating is what birthed me.

Trust

AUGUST 24, 2020

Trust,
That fickle antimatter;
Still, I subsidize.

Why is All the World Light

AUGUST 26, 2020

Why is all the world light and I am small underneath?
Just a black bottom under this apple tree?
Why am I in the limelight, the foreground?
The light pours no citrus drink, but a cyanide fruit pit pound!

The over-saturated curtains tail my frail feet.
Much busier than a yellow-black bee, bumping till its
stinger gets caught in a fabric hemming
and it dies with no one noticing.
The girl who reads, the tree that sifts its rotten leaves;
they care less, less for the discoloration that eats at me.

When the elders waltz the foxtrot dance so that even my
dwarf legs can follow suit,
I will never be quite slow, or fast enough?, for all of you.
I disintegrate daily into almost nothing.
I stare, but no one stares at me.

Oh, haven't I written a piece about shadows and light?
What's with me! I use the same machine work!
Metaphors, imageries, diction, diction mutating to a
deeper fiction. Unoriginal it is!
The masses cling onto clichés with their pointed teeth;
why can't I, I lodge into that all-inclusion?
Why do I repeat my own themes? Have I never learned
critical thinking?
I depend on repetition: same old, same old
(did I mention the old 'same'?)
thing to grasp any new concept!

Maladaptive daydreamer
who cannot conjure up any ink
of fresh difference! What purpose do I hold
in this awful, spineless world?
I am too awfully, awfully simple and dumb
to succeed in any other playing field!
Reality, what foreign entity is she?
Maybe a solemn quiet would do it for me.
(So maybe I'll have an extended vacation
and revisit my only talent some other day.)

What do the ~~sappy~~ honey-loving poets write on?
The ~~sawdust~~ stardust in eye pupils, and
igniting our hearts alight ~~till it guzzles that red stream~~
~~and we become only such and the carpet gets a free dye job.~~
Apparently, everything pure and worthy is atomized into
~~carbolic soap I allow carbonation of its soda acid in my~~
~~eyes~~ diamonds.

On atomic level substances,
let's rehearse the Compton effect:
Heat me up to a hundred keV
like cheap microwave dinner, so that I propel
and bang against metallic beings
till I decrease, and I fall powerless.
Each new orbit of opportunity I seize,
I result with less, and the opportunity snatches from me.
Glistening shoe shiner whose price tag appeals to the
average Joe,
then I swipe: scuffing up my rounded toe.

She tattooed the other girls' arrow on herself because:
"I'm pulled back to soar farther,"
yet this stretching has lasted for... months?
Compare this not to a crossbow, but to that of a
medieval rack, that gruesome torture device!
My tissue is tearing asunder, but this is polar from
breaking bread!
I ache, I ache, I ache! Isn't yoga supposed to tranquilize
you to a grounded state, not death?
Pop! Gush! Sprawled disorderly...

Why is the world so light when I am so heavy?
Why must I "lust for a life" that lusts not for me?

The Fears of My Thoughts

SEPTEMBER 1, 2020

Two cinquains.

Caffeine.
Nearing addict
Status; once spurned pure black
But now it's my composition.
Jitters

My thoughts;
Next round is scotch:
Next, I'm alcoholic.
Yet, withdrawal never latches.
I'm safe.

The Music of Caterpillars

SEPTEMBER 5, 2020

Swollen and obese: my head, my belly;
I'm frothed full of these in-betweens of tamborine slams
beneath my breastbone.
The bass drop is nigh, but it's mostly spacing.
Why do I rely on that kindling of hope
that someday the grain of noise will congeal
and it will lay simply, having my fingers twine overhead it?

The music of caterpillars, perhaps?
With their subtle leg pokes but monstrous main bodies.
I stuff myself with crumbs of the full tune
till I puke the leftovers—
oh, so myself.
"I don't want to be some *body*. I just want to be *me*."

I will never be *me*. She is a canvas portrait I sketched
with haste in my mind.

The Stars Mottle the View

SEPTEMBER 5, 2020

For a certain somebody...

Maybe I'll puke out my red innards, lungs and all:
I'm under the heavens, yet it's splotched with polar hues.

But ah! Stars! They subtly mottle the view.
This is the novel optimism I so craved.

Do I stand a chance to be such for him?
God contrived all: the white dots above me (but not yet for him); Hell beclouding the moon;
the sedulous twig contained in me, birching against my skin for dear life.
And our similar selves meeting.

I sit... longing for the future to unfold already.
God, I whisper, what is in your pre-release book of plans?
Will he and I interlock fingers? Will You rewrite the definition of intimacy for me?
~~Between the Lord and me.~~
This boy, (God's occupancy burrowed between), and me.

Perhaps he and I can admire your masterful art piece together,
the view of mottled white flecks.
Perhaps I'm here so he can embody the role of a rejector and shed off the *rejected*.
Perhaps I'm meant to be another rotting leftover so that he may completely heal.
Maybe — the choke slides through my esophagus —
we shall not interact years down the road.

Yet it's not up to me. So, I shall throw it all to Your embrace, and let you hammer up the nails in line.

I know so far:
This lovely boy, a soon to be man,
displays the points of my rightful traits to a lifelong partner:
Unafraid of his feminine, caressing me when I throw a fit, yet still a calm and collected voice of reason.

These words I write shall pass over his head:
as if he were laying on a beach playing dead,
the waves slobbering all over him, and he does not acknowledge it.
Maybe? Maybe not.
Will an awkward moment of realization linger in the humidity, or hibernate and blossom into an agreement?
Lord, I leave this in Your embrace.

The Way You Look Tonight (Isn't for Anyone to Wear)

SEPTEMBER 8, 2020

For my friends who cheer me up when they're feeling the most down: how do you do such? Why do you do such?

The way you look tonight is

so sullen, you 'con
artist', you 'caved-
in bygone'; that way
isn't right. You go to
and from the dichotomy: noon light and midnight.
Select one:
you're a savior ship rigged
intact to swoop me home safely, or the other:
you bare your fright, and your will
will never peak upright, for all of mankind's era.
May I inquire?
How do you equalize the balance scale?
The crippling illness brittles you
day in and day out, till you're it (me?) bit (me?) little.

Who's to blame... but
the manipulator, the roundest one:
life, life, life?
The mucus it achoos is diabetic, hon—;
eyeing the blades which pepper tic-tac-toe squares on the backs
of our throats.
We'll only ever be fresh
packaging from the market, never
browning to 'well-done'.

Let Me Spell It Out for You

SEPTEMBER 12, 2020

I was quarantined in a hotel room by orders from my workplace since I suspected I had coronavirus. Those ten days were blissful and a much-needed break from my toxic work environment. Upon returning to work, someone of authority inspected my room and exaggerated about a mess I had supposedly made in there. News of this reached my coworkers, and my anxiety exploded once again.

Screw you— yes, you on the towering stool, prettified
with zebra stripes.
I have had my reputation tainted by all mutated forms of
the disease. It does not exclude any race or gender.
Screw you— you unlocked the property gates and your
festering tongue drooled over all the houses.
Let me spell it out for you, not for the first or last time:

So, you lured me into a hotel room for free. No more
Countryside, that wasteland view, but a window to the
sea
Reefs, that bell dinging of 'home'. Ten days of
Elation, away from the drained-out mint gum: the
Warrior stadium for the modern gladiators.

You don't know this, but I am already that, continent
sized.
Oh, will her test score surpass the failing one? In
my own
Universe, I bombed it. This is the one instance I am
glad of such.

You could never get your fill, huh?
I frolic back into your wide arms, ready to face the dreaded workload.
"She trashed the room. Ungrateful little kid, she is."

Now every breathing thing wears outdated lenses:
to them, I'm saturated with zip zapping flies that birl past the highway speed limit so that I appear as a tumbleweed.

There you go again: winding the music box so I pirouette to the liars' national anthem.

Fuck you— you ruined my favorite song.

The Hell-Hounds

SEPTEMBER 19, 2020

After Sylvia Plath's 'I Am Vertical'

It's half past twelve into the new day.
Insomniac mutt, I slit a doggy door for you.
Come back home to your mother.
Trample me with your shoveled in dirt paws: you are elected for mayor.

Tie a knot on the leash.
Make space for a loopty-loop so my hourglass waist is a perfect fit.
Yank me away from my bed.

Throughout the day, I escape the wrath of your half-sisters, the hellhounds.
I greet with common sayings and set the timer at the perfect picosecond to conform to the molding mold:
the picometer of the worldly favor: content content.

I no longer aspire to be vertical; how laborious it really is.
The x-axis flattens the curve and coerces me to rest.
Those bloody hounds, they must weigh a ton.
They've warped spacetime in my blankets!
Why do they think they are God?

Exhaustion reigns all of me, the eventual winner.
So, I surrender and soar down into what they made.
The hounds cackle: "Let's pounce."
Their translucent heads ram me, so I tumble to the mattress's edge.
I should not be almost floating. I should not be almost floating.

To cope: I twiddle my frizz between my thumbs.
If I do this enough, split ends shall construct that ugly wishbone form.
Some more! Zipper up the hair shaft and reach my scalp and split that open too! Then to my middle! My toes!
Bloody hell hounds me every other hour, preventing proper sleep.

If I clock into work I shall be out of uniform.
Then they'll send me to a mental institution, and once I wear them out: the homeless shelter.

I don't even fit in with the misfits.
The only way to cleanse myself and not miss a wipe is to envelop in a nearby body
of water, but solely when it's dark out.
Daytime shan't accept me: I lie too horizontally.
To be squashed flat, to never revive: that is my calling.

Tsundaasaa (I'm Fine/ I'm Done For)

SEPTEMBER 25, 2020

I admitted myself to the emergency room after having especially strong suicidal thoughts the night prior. While staying in the ER, I drifted from feeling fine to feeling horrible. Worst of all, I felt my privacy was invaded the entire time.

I'm telling you, I'm fine:
Find me in the emergency room
with a braised nervous system.
Nervous but with brazen knuckles,
I saunter with my foot's heel hanging out of my shoe.

Find me trekking suddenly,
succumbing to blistering so I no longer rely on manmade soles.
The nurse tips me for coming, then taps at the keys:
"She's come here to die;
she's not made of 'man' anymore."

Surely, I'm done for:
They've undressed me of all my material,
the essence and the synthetic,
and now their hospital gown has claimed ownership of me.
The training nurses? the surgeons? the coworkers I had no clue walked this Earth?

angle the door to catch a view of my barely adult bare everything.
They slither a needle in my comfort bubble, easing in then out.
They observe the strange nutcase, the new specimen.

I'm okay, duh.
I don't need my mommy here; I morphed into her beta prototype.
So why is your jaw hanging? Are you that shocked? The only electricity found here is the overhead light. Are you that desperate for an electron surge to pang against you?

I know I do. I'm doomed.
Yeah, we can tell you're in distress, but we need that random guy's number. Just routine paperwork things.

Oh numbers— they come from math, I think?
They're like their own alphabet. Oh quick!—
Pen it down! Give yourself a tattoo, now!
Prod prod prod the conoid so deep that the pen becomes a new limb. I'm a daring woman: impale—

Tsundaasaa! The uchina has burst forth!
Yet any crumb of her culture has been drained from the dishwasher.

Tsundaasaa! What is she even uttering?
She was never meant to enter such a typhoon contraption.

Blanched and bland, she is atrophying into minced garlic, genetically modified.
What is she then? What was she then?
A lost cause, obviously.

Doc, send her off.

*uchina – Okinawan female

Art Therapy

SEPTEMBER 27, 2020

One of two poems I wrote during my stay at a psychiatric unit. I describe the picture I drew from one of the art therapy classes.

I conjured forth a desert.
In my rectangular view, it is less than a quarter of it all.
Smear its sand across the page, redefine where the equator should be,
that tinge of life I've been shooed away from.

In its middle lane it droops!
Like a sagging granny's under eyes.
Quicksand in this arid land—
Wait stop! What have we here?
An iris's petals unfurl out of it. They cradle the young in them.
I, the spin top girl, shall undo the whirl.

A ladder, strong from food and sturdy in every fibrous twig,
shoots to the tallest fly high level,
a smidge apart from palace sky, my chosen family's address.
Yet there on the wobbling rungs, I have hung the barb.
(I tried beguiling my vision. They glint from fairy lights.
—No, who am I fooling? It's all metal.)
Their frays shear even my intangible will,
shoving me down. Gating me out.
I neighbor the ground more than the ups.
I'm discordant with anything above eye level.

The horseflesh tots through the bottom left.
Once was my partner-in-crime, titling me a cowgirl.

Now he's indecisive and directionless, the stupid rocking horse he truly is.
His cornea circumference cuts, opens its jelly mouth wide and bawls some cherry flesh out of them.
He rounds up his stringy spit into a curd
then aims a cannonball blow to

the Rubik's cube.
Three by three, uniform in color code; this is my standard.
A remorseless set of fingers shall torque every square, every center,
leaving me no hints for a head start.
I admit, I raise my hands to your handcuff.
I've no recollection of original alignment.
Where is the end?

Heartbreak Hotel

SEPTEMBER 29, 2020

The second poem I wrote during my stay at a psychiatric unit. I had read about a prisoner of war (POW) who was confined at the Heartbreak Hotel during the Vietnam War.

Prisoner of war, the bottommost level of being.
How could a second hand ever reach?

I have done my noblest of dues
and this is the scrap I receive?
Doing time with the hideous,
the sucked clean lemon slices,
littering this algae ridden floor.

As if extraneous baubles from the sun's appearance could disperse this muddy fog...
Fungi on my excrement: this is now my diet.

I revolve the gears of my watch counterclockwise:
I'm in the interrogation room. My spine is straight.
Patrice, she sits across.

"It's recording now. Just so I know my ears aren't failing me,
you say you planned to stuff yourself with pills, like a toymaker stuffs his teddies with cotton balls?"

Rumor has it, one is given a life sentence when they take matters into their own hands.
I wonder whose brilliant mind conceived such a law.
Don't the convicted go to Hell?
And the ones who fail: Heartbreak Hotel?

Yet in this chain of the franchise,
I am treated with grace and forbearance.
My head can crash land on my pillow with no trepidations of liars waiting at the bus stop to capture me.

Oh! But on the day of release...
Shall I waddle to the second version once more?
The employees will lure me, play their royalty-free kitten purrs till I stand before the door.
It'll bribe me: "Shelter! Your true home is here!
Welcome to the last day of your life!"
Will I carry the sufficient vigor to object?

Life — chance — and all your outdoors:
My clumsy fingers grab at you again!

He is All Love

OCTOBER 9, 2020

How it felt to be rejected a second time. I felt ashamed for being vulnerable with someone again.

I shall suffer in secret—
in a triumphant, grandiose quiet.
I shall suffer, shriek an utter, then muffle the gunshot.

It's coming soon.
I write these tender bits onto this page and pray that I won't be snatched mid-sentence
and creased into an origami fold, beheaded, then crucified.
But no— the detonation is coming soon.

I shall rage in the autumn dirt, wilt my final leaves, and bury beneath the sugar powdered snow.
Once I'm in the lost and found, he'll blame himself and himself alone.

Passion is shameful. Passion is crude.
Passion is my genetic pool. Passion is a fool.
Love delights not in evil. Love rejoices with the truth:
「No offense, but we are too dissimilar, so unlike.
I am all Love. We could never meet.」

I rub in that spoiled, milky lotion of certainty.
Well, I'll be damned: my skin remains crusted and parched.
I'm stiff.
I'm forbidden to prance like the musical protagonist I once dressed as.

To Embrace (Without Pain)

OCTOBER 15, 2020

A response to my poem 'The Most Admirable Trait'. Forgiving is easier said than done. For years I had guilted myself for not being able to forgive certain people who emotionally neglected me, but trauma is difficult to bandage. If it takes me a year, twenty years, or never to forgive, that's okay. God is quick to forgive, but we will never be Him. Take your time. Set a comfortable pace.

A lifetime of livid seething
is only a microscopic contusion to the Creator.

Swallowing clemency in its whole is great and all, but
some like to chew slowly on clementine fruits.
My molars bounce on their lipids and hole-punch
through them.
In its succession, the tanginess flows, ripples, and drifts.
The sour outside squirms my tongue to a spasm, flips a
light switch in my mouth, and reveals the forgotten
fructose.

My Father despises deluding hares, the quick-to-the-
finish-liners.
I am the tortoise: slowly but surely, I warm myself up to
forgiveness — the definition and all its synonyms — then
I befriend it.

To embrace without pain is the aim I shall seek.
Oh, what if it takes me till I reach the brink of mortality?
What if I never rip off the leech?
That is valid, that is fine: He knows that is honesty.

5D

OCTOBER 24, 2020

I am
the highway tunnels drilled in your gums
from when your baby teeth plucked themselves out.

I am
the slut rotting on the bed,
whose gelatin you flayed off with your rusted spoon.

I am
the accused with his bounty price
plastered across the billboard sign.

I am
the dying fetus
jutting her head outside the womb.

I am these tributaries — these waves that thirst — which,
at first glance, don't connect. In time, they will prove

that humanity has claimed territory in them.
I am the mouth, drooling forth my mountain water.

This larger lake! I shall never see beyond it.
I am not the fifth dimension, where the sky hangs its
hook.

So what?
I have its might. I am the colonizer in its territory,
and I claim it.

Perhaps I Should Control This Birth

NOVEMBER 7, 2020

The man in the white coat— yes, you!
My mind is fraught; I task you a soot-filled deed:
Package up my worst fears
— who? a man's bundle of joy —
silly string me till you rue the job:

Crowbar December's lips agape.
Do the irreversible: have its breath salt-preserve my
tubes and manifest in me a gory version of a single strand
knot.
Good sir, while you're at it: shut the rest of the system
down. Sew it tight with your girthiest thread.
Stick a velvet bow atop it.

Only then could I hope
to be the model nun, the faultless monk—
a guaranteed pure woman who could never stain
anything with her cursed mark.
My ears are failing me— I hear the gurgles and the hums.
Winter wants so badly to waltz out of the womb.
Its shrapnel grinds at my organ walls!
Acid etch this carnivorous flesh
inside me. Fray it till it softens to feathers.

If I call you my darling,
will you cook up some breakfast so I'm no longer full
from digesting you?
If I feed you, little wrecking ball,
will you remain swaying on the back-porch swing?
Don't even think about coming down, nightmarish freak.

The Annual Black Breath

November 10, 2020

I swirl into myself.

I fold,

I fold,

then I crimp

into an unnatural pose.

Air's knuckles knock.
Should I answer?
"Resuscitate her." "Wake up."
Well, wait.
Let me consider such a weighty ultimatum.

Life, I have just one question:
Why give me nourishment when in the next hour, you
somehow muddy, mutilate, murder, and massacre my
drinking water?
On second thought, I have a few more:

Why give?
Me?
Nourishment when?
The next?
(How?) Our?
You? Some? How?
muddy, mutilate, murder, and massacre?
muddymutilatemurdermassacremuddymutilatemurder
my drinking? water?

The answer will never land.
The annual black breath steals the lead role once again.

The eye of the hurricane twist is the truth holder.
A living hand could not ever reach it.

Fellow people and any creature still sagging around some blood-bloated parts:

Nothing is as it seems, even when we are misguided in believing we have grasped the 'concept'.
Sense. Answers. Answer this:
was it ever meant to be?

I Hear They Never Rest

DECEMBER 13, 2020

I suppose 'tis the season.
Can I chase with my strained, yet toned, calves?
How must I maintain my running start?
Buoy my rollicking boat?
Answer: I sing a spell. I reinvent the principles of physics.
I am now an alchemist; I alter my form:

The steaming sewage from my veins always tries to wash the wreck, but I have divorced my cast!
My toes pluck out the pebbles and I ram myself into the garden's grit.
Behold! The neighborhood's tree: lacking vegetation but somehow still standing!

I would hate to be a human. I'm told they never rest.
We 'slackers' stamp ourselves in the freezer's cotton and we hibernate. No test in our wooly vest.

Do I miss the miscreant who promised a neverland,
then dumped me into his mouth, gargling me around?
I don't see why I should.

Plus, he lurks even when we are free.
He swaddles his legs around our torsos,
thinking he is the passenger, and we are his joyride.

Let's ignore his tyranny for now, shall we?

'Tis the season to be impossible,
to keep myself under wraps.

The Solutions

DECEMBER 15, 2020

At last! The apex away from the valley!
No agony here. Trauma is now an obsolete term.
An old wives' tale. You know nothing of it.
Here, you're in need of some nutrition.
Take some of this food. Trust me on this.

Bite. Let it slip down, but not all the way.
What's stuck in your throat?
An animal's femur? An Adam's apple?
It's a new pair hands: they strangle you,
but they won't let you die today.
The fingernails scrape, then grate, your chords.
The gag reflex triggers.
Your teeth drape like weighty curtains, speeding up your body's age.

Describe your symptoms, young lady.
I'm waiting.
Have you nothing to say? I'll prescribe these, then:
Therapists. Friends with false faces. Family?
The typical trinkets to tinker with. Seek refuge in them.
They'll add some pressure to your wound.
It hurts? It hurts?
Why? They're only doing what they can!

Answer the following in explicit detail, from start to finish:
Do you devote everything to your see-through God?
Did you pluck every string in your heart for Him
Till your fingertips tore skin, then calloused up?
Did you pray your laments before you broke
Your fast? (A secret: I hear Christ is deaf.)

Once you picked up your spoon, did you scoop
in every fresh air source that could ever exist?
Stretch?
Nearly fracture several joints while you were at it?
Have you? Well, have you?
Her language decayed before civilization birthed Latin.
Or maybe she isn't quite right in the head.
She must be brain dead. We already explained this:
No agony here. Trauma is now an obsolete term.
An old wives' tale. You know nothing of it.

Whatever is the matter with you?

You Are Not My Eater

DECEMBER 19, 2020

Even within this bathtub,
The most constricting space,
I could not evade you.

My razor blade barely culls the cornfield on my limbs.
That pathetic excuse of a cutter sufficed little as a
hole puncher;
Optimistic I was for its penny tarnish to sicken me.

No need for that: you were the executioner.
Invade, invade... maim her!
O, but slow one, this is the scene:

My bodily sap had teemed out the faucet,
Brimming the cup full
Of boiling black milk, my monsoon erosion.

Cast iron skillet, this concave crib—
Half-orbs bloom in the drink, impregnating solid air.
In their wombs, I hammer in lungs which circulate
my breath.

Are you bewitched, arch nemesis?
Believe it with your pair of protruding pupils:
Futile one, you crashed the corpse party.

The eyesore, I am! Still, you yearn to trot on my acres,
To see me barren. Dip your toes.
See how that goes. Can you handle a Sun that's
liquid in form?

Whimper your dubbed puppy cry.
Affirm those lies: that I am a sauna one warms up
To over time.

The plug has been pulled, you self-absorbed judge.
My bone-thick lattice plays peekaboo in the pipes.
A phalanx reels in the hook. I swallow whole.

Cuts Are A Cyst

DECEMBER 23, 2020

I am not with you, my Ryukyu island.
We have divorced, but with great remorse.
My ear canals grovel this insistent grain instead:

in waves, these freedom men swarm,
their beer bellies ebb and flow.
So adamant! I hate it, so:
'Girls live in the dressing room! Go and give our look a try.'

I hide. For a moment we had our separate coffins.
The boss-battle was over with.
O, the ditz I am!
The men had conglomerated into protein.
Dead, then revived.
A hefty lash plunges into my sun-dried eye
of the hurricane. I am to remain calm amidst this peril.

Catharsis— read the word by each meter, each block.
Cut, cut! Cuts
are a cyst. This is all a system.

Catharsis: a fictitious term.
My dictionary surely doesn't acknowledge it.

The crowd, the crowd!
Look at these irritants, they are all just rabid dogs.
They won't stop their barking. Who's coming in?

Up next is the bitch. She struts with her preppy limp,
stripper heels and all. I may have seen her before.

She arrives as if she is the indicator of the new work
day. From which city, which state
does this manner originate? Not from yours,
truly.
I stand front and center
on their Japanese flag.
I am merely the depopulated red
and these blinding men are the white

steel, armored, encircling me.
They huddle ‘round, prepped for
the satanic ritual
which will sizzle corrosion at my rim.
The bait is abated!

Or so the legend goes.

AFTERWORD

And so, we arrive to the conclusion of my first poetry collection.

What you are holding in your hands is something valuable. I pride myself on never being afraid to display my vulnerability on the page, so I will prove that ability with the proceeding words: I edged so close to ending my own life a few times before self-publishing this. That may have been apparent given the content of some of the poems in here, but to be even more frank, the main motivator for me to finish out this task and title myself an author was that once I finally achieved my one real desire in life – publishing this work – I could end my life with no major regrets. This book is obviously a prize for me, but I think for anyone who decides this book was worthy of a purchase or a borrow, it really is a gem. No, I am not trying to boast.

A few months prior to publishing this, I said to myself, "To hell with this. Nothing I do will make me happy. Not even publishing my collection, because what follows that achievement is feeling pure nothing. Why should I keep living when that's the fact?"

I won't say that I have overridden that belief. I still unwillingly cling to it with overwhelming shame. Of course, I am proud of myself for slaving away many hours into developing this body of work, yet as of this point: any major steps I take to transfigure my life into all I've ever wanted has me land me back to the horror-filled disappointment I was trying to escape in the first place. One could argue it's because my state of mind hasn't changed. I won't deny that, but I also think it's because too often, I romanticize what life could be for me and the results are far from what I envisioned.

Viewing life through rose-tinted glasses isn't always a terrible idea, however. That might be what helps one stay sane for a time. Balance buoys us through life but locating the perfect middle point is what is so difficult. Maybe we are not meant to know where it is and depending on what stage of life you're in, that balance lands in a different spot. It's as if once we have a grasp on the answer, it flees elsewhere.

It is both insanity and an awe to never know balance by heart.

To provide some form of relief, may this collection help you in any way. Even if you only enjoyed one poem in here.

It's astonishing that this collection started with my eyes and my eyes only looking at it. Fifteen-year-old me isolated herself in her bedroom to avoid the wrath of an emotionally abusive father while also mourning the lack of communication from her mother, who was a thousand miles away. I wrote my first few poems as an act of rebellion: a silent opposition against the wrongs of my environment.

Only my Notes app knew of this secret hobby of mine. The app was my main confidante, the sole listener of my troubles and confusion of the world. Yet, I was determined to have this book reach a larger audience. I would copy and paste the work from my Notes app to a Google Doc and as time passed, it amounted to over two hundred pages. Many poems I adore (and some I cringe at) did not end up in the collection, but nonetheless I am proud that I expressed myself through them all.

I already have a page of dedications in the first few pages of this collection, but two people I forgot to mention is the poet Erin Hanson and singer-songwriter Tori Amos.

Before I stumbled across Erin's work, I disliked poetry. I did not understand the purpose of it. Then, a few days before I planned to commit suicide at age thirteen, one of her poems popped up on my Pinterest homepage. I read and read all the poems signed off with 'e.h' and felt some of the burden lifted off me. Her work proved to me that I was not alone in my suffering and in feeling unlovable. Her work also reinforced that I inherently have worth. Each line in a poem was a finger interlocking with my own, holding me in support so that I wouldn't plummet all the way down. Even if I were to fall – and I surely would as the years progressed – I wouldn't be the only one at the bottom. Erin's work literally saved my life, all because she chose to share her vulnerabilities to the public. I wouldn't have even consumed poetry and two years later, produced it, if it were not for her.

Lastly, to Tori Amos: when my own mother's presence was practically erased, I found your music and felt the touch of a mother's embrace again. Your lyricism has had a major influence on my own writing style but above all, through your art I felt love. I felt heard. Thank you so much.

Do not be afraid to share what you create. Even if you must go anonymous, humanity needs to see it. You may feel insignificant, or that your expression isn't the best; but, if it comes from the heart, people will sense that.

Nobody's voice is too meek to be heard. After all, the deaf can still feel vibrations rippling through their bodies. So, speak to your heart's content. It is a necessity.

Sammi Yamashiro
March 10, 2021

About Sammi Yamashiro

Sammi Yamashiro was born in Okinawa, Japan in 2001. She spent much of her childhood there, apart from the one year she lived in Marshall Islands when she was fifteen and sixteen. There, she started writing poetry and has continued since. She currently lives in Virginia.